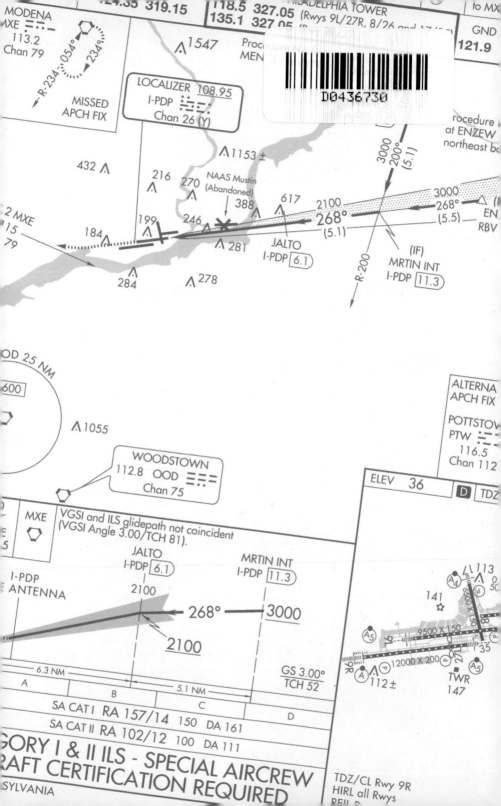

MODENA
MXE ▪ ▬ ▪ ▪
113.2
Chan 79
R-234···054°
234°

MISSED
APCH FIX

124.35 319.15

118.5 327.05
135.1 327.05

▲ 1547

PHILADELPHIA TOWER
(Rwys 9L/27R, 8/26 and 17...)

to MX

GND
121.9

Proce...
MEN

LOCALIZER 108.95
I-PDP ▪ ▬ ▪ ▬ ▪
Chan 26 (Y)

D0436730

rocedure
at ENZEW
northeast b...

432 ▲

▲ 1153 ±

216
▲

270
▲

NAAS Mustin
(Abandoned)
388
▲

617
▲

2100

3000
200°
(5.1)

3000

268°
EN
RBV

2 MXE
15
79

184 ▲

199
▲

246
▲

281
▲

268°
(5.1)

268°
(5.5)

JALTO
I-PDP 6.1

(IF)
MRTIN INT
I-PDP 11.3

R-200

284 ▲

▲ 278

OD 25 NM

600

▲ 1055

WOODSTOWN
112.8 OOD ▬ ▬ ▬
Chan 75

ALTERNA
APCH FIX

POTTSTOW
PTW ▪ ▬ ▪ ▬
116.5
Chan 112

ELEV 36

D TDZ

MXE
◇

VGSI and ILS glidepath not coincident
(VGSI Angle 3.00/TCH 81).

JALTO
I-PDP 6.1

MRTIN INT
I-PDP 11.3

113

141
☆

I-PDP
ANTENNA

2100

268°

3000

2100

9500 X 150

12000 X 200

35

9R
112 ±

TWR
147

6.3 NM

A

B

5.1 NM

C

GS 3.00°
TCH 52

D

SA CAT I RA 157/14 150 DA 161

SA CAT II RA 102/12 100 DA 111

GORY I & II ILS - SPECIAL AIRCREW
RAFT CERTIFICATION REQUIRED

SYLVANIA

TDZ/CL Rwy 9R
HIRL all Rwys
REIL

208°	Apt Elev	36

uires specific OPSPEC, MSPEC or LOA approval and use of HUD to DH.
duced lighting: requires specific OPSPEC, MSPEC or LOA
use of autoland or HUD to touchdown.

MALSR

(A5)

MISSED APPROACH: Climb
1500 then climbing right tur
3000 on MXE VORTAC R-1
to MXE VORTAC and hold.

PHILADELPHIA APP CON	PHILADELPHIA TOWER		GND CON	CLNC D
124.35 319.15	118.5 327.05 (Rwys 9L/27R, 8/26 and 17/35)		121.9 348.6	118.85 3
	135.1 327.05 (Rwy 9R/27L)			

CPDLC

Procedure NA for arrivals at
MENGE on V479 northbound.

∧ 1547

(IAF)
MENGE
ARD [15]

108.2 ARD
Chan 19

Procedure NA for arrivals
at ENZEW on V123-157-2
northeast bound.

LOCALIZER 108.95
I-PDP ⋮−⋮⋮.
Chan 26 (Y)

MISSED
APCH FIX

3000
200°
(5.1)

∧ 1153 ±

3000
268°
(5.5)

(IAF)
ENZEW
RBV [23.1]

088°

432 ∧

216 ∧   270 ∧

NAAS Mustin
(Abandoned)
388 ∧

617 ∧   2100
268°
(5.1)

(IF)
MRTIN INT
I-PDP [11.3]

246

JALTO
I-PDP [6.1]

199 ∧

∧ 281

R-200

184 ∧

∧ 278

∧ 284

25 NM

∧ 1055

00

WOODSTOWN
112.8 OOD ≡⋮≡
Chan 75

ALTERNATE MIS
APCH FIX

POTTSTOWN
PTW ⋮−−
116.5
Chan 112

ELEV 36   D   TDZE

000

MXE ◇

VGSI and ILS glidepath not coincident
(VGSI Angle 3.00/TCH 81).

MRTIN INT
I-PDP [11.3]

∧ 113

MXE
R-115

JALTO
I-PDP [6.1]
2100

(A4)
141 ☆

I-PDP
DME ANTENNA

268°

3000

9500 X 150

2100

(A5)

12000 X 200

GS 3.00°
TCH 52

9R
(A) 112 ±

TWR
147

81'

	6.3 NM	5.1 NM	
RY	A	B	C	D

SA CAT I RA 157/14 150 DA 161

SA CAT II RA 102/12 100 DA 111

NERVES
OF STEEL

YOUNG READERS EDITION

268° | Apt Elev 36

MALSR

MISSED APPROACH: Climb to
1500 then climbing right
3000 on MXE VORTAC R
to MXE VORTAC and hol

requires specific OPSPEC, MSPEC or LOA approval and use of HUD to DH.
Reduced lighting: requires specific OPSPEC, MSPEC or LOA
and use of autoland or HUD to touchdown.

A₅

| PHILADELPHIA APP CON 124.35 319.15 | PHILADELPHIA TOWER 118.5 327.05 (Rwys 9L/27R, 8/26 and 17/35) 135.1 327.05 (Rwy 9R/27L) | GND CON 121.9 348.6 | CLNC 118.85 |

CPD

Procedure NA for arrivals at
MENGE on V479 northbound.

108.2 ARD
Chan 19

(IAF)
MENGE
ARD 15

Procedure NA for arrivals
at ENZEW on V123-157-
northeast bound.

∧1547

054°
234°

3000
200°
(5.1)

LOCALIZER 108.95
I-PDP
Chan 26 (Y)

3000
268°
(5.5)

088°

(IAF)
ENZEW
RBV 23.1

MISSED
APCH FIX

∧1153 ±

NAAS Mustin
(Abandoned)

2100
268°
(5.1)

432 ∧

216
∧

270
∧

388

617
∧

R-200

(IF)
MRTIN INT
I-PDP 11.3

199
∧

246

∧ 281

JALTO
I-PDP 6.1

184∧

∧
284

∧ 278

ALTERNATE M
APCH FIX

POTTSTOWN
PTW
116.5
Chan 112

OD 25 NM

2600

∧1055

ELEV 36

D TDZ

WOODSTOWN
112.8 OOD
Chan 75

141
☆

A₄

9500 X 150

A₅

3000

MXE

VGSI and ILS glidepath not coincident
(VGSI Angle 3.00/TCH 81).

MRTIN INT
I-PDP 11.3

12000 X 200

MXE
R-115

JALTO
I-PDP 6.1

3000

A 112 ±

TW
147

2100

268°

I-PDP
DME ANTENNA

2100

GS 3.00°
TCH 52

	6.3 NM		5.1 NM	
1181'	A	B	C	D
ORY				
27R	SA CAT I RA 157/14 150 DA 161			

LOS GATOS LIBRARY

LOS GATOS, CALIFORNIA

NERVES OF STEEL

YOUNG READERS EDITION

The Incredible True Story of How One
Woman Followed Her Dreams, Stayed
True to Herself, and Saved 148 Lives

CAPTAIN TAMMIE JO SHULTS

THOMAS NELSON
Since 1798

Nerves of Steel Young Readers Edition

© 2019 Echo Four Fourteen, LLC

All rights reserved. No portion of this book may be reproduced, stored in a retrieval system, or transmitted in any form or by any means—electronic, mechanical, photocopy, recording, scanning, or other—except for brief quotations in critical reviews or articles, without the prior written permission of the publisher.

Published in Nashville, Tennessee, by Tommy Nelson. Tommy Nelson is an imprint of Thomas Nelson. Thomas Nelson is a registered trademark of HarperCollins Christian Publishing, Inc.

Cover and infographic design by Greg Jackson of ThinkPen Design.

Tommy Nelson titles may be purchased in bulk for educational, business, fund-raising, or sales promotional use. For information, please e-mail SpecialMarkets@ ThomasNelson.com.

The names and identifying characteristics of certain individuals have been changed to protect their privacy.

Any Internet addresses (websites, blogs, etc.) printed in this book are offered as a resource and are not intended in any way to be or to imply an endorsement by Thomas Nelson, nor does Thomas Nelson vouch for the existence, content, or services of these sites beyond the life of this book.

Library of Congress Cataloging-in-Publication Data

Names: Shults, Tammie Jo, 1961- author.
Title: Nerves of steel : the incredible true story of how one woman followed her
    dreams, stayed true to herself, and saved 148 lives / Captain Tammie Jo Shults.
Description: Young readers edition. | Nashville, Tennessee, USA : Thomas Nelson,
    [2019] | Includes bibliographical references. | Audience: Ages 8-12 | Audience:
    Grades 4-6 | Summary: "The amazing story of pilot Tammie Jo Shults, adapted
    for young readers! Tammie Jo worked hard, had faith, stayed true to herself, and
    overcame every obstacle on her journey to becoming a navy pilot. Years later,
    those lessons served her well as she was put in the right place at the right time to
    safely land a crippled plane and save 148 lives"-- Provided by publisher.
Identifiers: LCCN 2019034271 (print) | LCCN 2019034272 (ebook) | ISBN
    9781400215317 (hardcover) | ISBN 9781400215300 (paperback) | ISBN
    9781400216673 (epub)
Subjects: LCSH: Shults, Tammie Jo, 1961---Juvenile literature. | Air pilots--United
    States--Biography--Juvenile literature. | Aircraft accidents--United States--Juvenile
    literature.
Classification: LCC TL540.S476 A3 2019 (print) | LCC TL540.S476 (ebook) | DDC
    363.12/4092 [B]--dc23
LC record available at https://lccn.loc.gov/2019034271
LC ebook record available at https://lccn.loc.gov/2019034272

Printed in the United States of America

19 20 21 22 23   PC/LSCC   10 9 8 7 6 5 4 3 2 1

Mfr: PC/LSCC / Crawfordsville, IN / October 2019 / PO #9553792

To the brave hearts aboard Flight 1380, and to the extraordinary team of professionals that supported us that day, both in the air and on the ground.

He, who, from zone to zone,
Guides through the boundless sky thy certain
    flight,
In the long way that I must trace alone,
Will lead my steps aright.

WILLIAM CULLEN BRYANT, "TO A WATERFOWL"

CONTENTS

| 268° | Apt Elev | 36 | | |

requires specific OPSPEC, MSPEC or LOA approval and use of HUD to DH.
educed lighting: requires specific OPSPEC, MSPEC or LOA
d use of autoland or HUD to touchdown.

MALSR	MISSED APPROACH: Clir 1500 then climbing right 3000 on MXE VORTAC R to MXE VORTAC and hol

A5

PHILADELPHIA APP CON 124.35 319.15	PHILADELPHIA TOWER 118.5 327.05 (Rwys 9L/27R, 8/26 and 17/35) 135.1 327.05 (Rwy 9R/27L)	GND CON 121.9 348.6	CLNC 118.85
			CPDL

Procedure NA for arrivals at
MENGE on V479 northbound.

054°
234°

A1547

(IAF)
MENGE
ARD 15

108.2 ARD
Chan 19

Procedure NA for arrivals
at ENZEW on V123-157-
northeast bound.

LOCALIZER 108.95
I-PDP
Chan 26 (Y)

3000
200°
(5.1)

3000
268°
(5.5)

088°
(IAF)
ENZEW
RBV 23.1

MISSED
APCH FIX

A1153 ±

NAAS Mustin
(Abandoned)

432 A

216 A   270 A

617 A
388 A

2100
268°
(5.1)

(IF)
MRTIN INT
I-PDP 11.3

JALTO
I-PDP 6.1

199 A   246 A
A 281

R-200

184 A

A 278

A 284

ALTERNATE M
APCH FIX

POTTSTOWN
PTW
116.5
Chan 112

D 25 NM

600

A1055

ELEV   36   D   TDZE

WOODSTOWN
112.8 OOD
Chan 75

VGSI and ILS glidepath not coincident
(VGSI Angle 3.00/TCH 81).

3000

MXE

MXE
R-115

JALTO
I-PDP 6.1

MRTIN INT
I-PDP 11.3

141

I-PDP
DME ANTENNA

2100

268°

2100

3000

9500 X 150

GS 3.00°
TCH 52

12000 X 200

TWR
147

181'

	6.3 NM		5.1 NM	
	A	B	C	D

ORY

SA CAT I RA 157/14 150 DA 161

27R

RA 102/12 100 DA 111

PROLOGUE

April 17, 2018

New York's LaGuardia Airport is a bit tricky for airline pilots. LGA, as we call it, can be like quicksand—easy to get stuck in. Fortunately today is not one of those days, and it looks like my first officer and I are going to escape the LGA trap without any worries.

Our plane pushes back from the gate on time, and we taxi out to runway 31 and are cleared for takeoff without having to pause. It's First Officer Darren Ellisor's turn to fly, so I get us lined up and give him the controls. He pushes the *throttles* up, and we're off. The city quickly falls away below us. We point our nose southwest and settle in for a four-hour flight to Dallas Love Field in Texas. What a beautiful day to fly!

But about twenty minutes into the flight, as we climb

to 32,500 feet over eastern Pennsylvania, this beautiful day turns ugly.

BOOM!

Something explodes like an artillery shell, and it feels like our plane has been hit. A quick look at the *cockpit* gauges tells me our left engine is dead. This isn't good, but it's manageable. (I've been practicing single-engine failures in the flight *simulator* for twenty-four years.)

A fraction of a second later, "not good" becomes "not good at all." The jet, a Boeing 737–700, quickly rolls off to the left. The nose jerks hard and drops into a dive. Darren and I both lunge for the controls. Something more than an engine failure has happened, but what? Then a bone-jarring shudder runs through the aircraft. Chaos takes over.

The air pressure plummets, and Darren and I can't breathe. Just as the air is sucked out of our lungs, the air-conditioning system pulls gray smoke into the cockpit. A sharp pain pierces our ears. A deafening roar floods our heads. We can't hear anything else. The plane vibrates so hard that our instruments become a crazy blur. An incredible, invisible power continues to pull our 737 toward the earth. We've never practiced *this* in the simulator.

First, we need our oxygen masks.

Amid the confusion, time seems to slow down. I can't see, I can't hear, and I can't breathe. My heart races, but my thoughts become very clear: *This isn't the first time*

I've been in an out-of-control aircraft. It isn't the first time I've flown without all the information I need. It isn't the first time I've brushed up against disaster.

This is a good news–bad news situation. The bad news first: I'm not sure the left wing can take much more of the abuse caused by the exploded engine and its damage. This might be the day I meet my Maker face-to-face.

The good news? We're still flying. It's time to get to work.

requires specific OPSPEC, MSPEC or LOA approval and use of HUD to DH.
educed lighting: requires specific OPSPEC, MSPEC or LOA
d use of autoland or HUD to touchdown.

| MALSR |
| A5 |

MISSED APPROACH: Clin
1500 then climbing right
3000 on MXE VORTAC R
to MXE VORTAC and hol

PHILADELPHIA APP CON 124.35 319.15	PHILADELPHIA TOWER		GND CON 121.9 348.6	CLNC 118.85
	118.5 327.05 (Rwys 9L/27R, 8/26 and 17/35)			
	135.1 327.05 (Rwy 9R/27L)			CPDL

Procedure NA for arrivals at MENGE on V479 northbound.

Procedure NA for arrivals at ENZEW on V123-157-northeast bound.

∧1547

(IAF) MENGE ARD 15

108.2 ARD
Chan 19

3000 200° (5.1)

3000 268° (5.5)

088°

(IAF) ENZEW RBV 23.1

MISSED APCH FIX

LOCALIZER 108.95
I-PDP
Chan 26 (Y)

∧1153 ±

432 ∧

216 ∧   270 ∧
NAAS Mustin (Abandoned)
388

617 ∧   2100 268° (5.1)

JALTO I-PDP 6.1

(IF) MRTIN INT I-PDP 11.3

R-200

199 ∧   246
∧ 281

184 ∧

∧ 278
284 ∧

ALTERNATE M APCH FIX

POTTSTOWN PTW
116.5
Chan 112

D 25 NM

600

∧1055

WOODSTOWN
112.8 OOD
Chan 75

ELEV 36   D   TDZE

∧11
A4   ∧
141 ☆

VGSI and ILS glidepath not coincident (VGSI Angle 3.00/TCH 81).

3000
MXE
MXE R-115

MRTIN INT I-PDP 11.3

A5

12000 X 200

JALTO I-PDP 6.1

I-PDP DME ANTENNA

2100

268°

2100

3000

GS 3.00°
TCH 52

A4 112±

TWR
147

181'
RY
7R

6.3 NM

5.1 NM

	A	B	C	D

SA CAT I RA 157/14 150 DA 161
SA CAT II RA 102/12 100 DA 111

NO SECOND-CLASS CITIZENS

My earliest memories are of wide-open skies. Big and blue, they sprawled over the small town of Farmington, New Mexico, where I was born in 1961. The gorgeous sun set and the bright moon rose over high, flat mesas that looked as if they'd been painted with watercolors. I guess most of my memories are of what was above me because when you're little, you're always looking up.

I looked up to my parents first. As I started school, they moved our family to a five-acre farm near Florida Mesa, Colorado, in the southwest corner of the state. Dad worked there as a grader operator, building country roads and making ski slopes for a nearby resort. My dad was tall and could whistle like no one else I knew. These were superhero qualities in my eyes.

Mom was always cooking or canning our home-grown vegetables, milking cows, or feeding chickens. She also sewed most of my sister's and my clothes. If we needed a tractor driver while we loaded hay, then she drove the tractor too.

Dwight was my older brother by thirteen months. Sandra, my sister, was born a year and a half after me. From the beginning, we knew Sandra wasn't like everyone else. But we didn't know until she was nine that she had cerebral palsy, a disorder that affects a person's muscle movements and brain development.

Mom and Dad sold the cream from our cows' milk to buy piano lessons, a true luxury, for Dwight and me. The day we got our piano was the first day we heard our mom play. It was drop-your-lunch-pail beautiful, even to a first grader.

Each day we had to practice before we could go out to play. Mom sweetened her practice-before-play rule by saying, "Piano practice will make your fingers faster. You'll be able to catch more frogs." In our home, you could change instruments, but you could never quit. Sandra didn't play the piano, but she loved to sing with others. Drawing and needlework were her style of fun.

Dad seemed to always be working. But he found time

to make child-size wooden guitars from strips of plywood, nails, and thin, silver wire. Dwight, Sandra, and I took these treasures to our hideouts, where we strummed and sang as if it sounded good.

Childhood was happy because my family was happy. We lived simply on our farm, raising our crops, tending livestock, and being fed by both. We were always raising a pig and a calf, usually undersized runts.

One of the runt pigs we took under wing was especially cute and clever. She loved to chew gum! When given a piece, she would pace and stamp at the screen door of our house with impatient little grunts, wanting to be let in. The family would gather for the show, then open the door while one of us gave a running commentary on the little pig's actions. After trotting in, she would set her haunches down in the middle of the hallway rug, put her nose straight up in the air, and smack loudly with her eyes closed. When the flavor was gone, she'd spit out the gum and head back outside.

When it came to chores, Dwight and I both bucked bales of hay on and off the hay trailer, mucked out stalls and fertilized the garden, milked cows, and mended fences. When we were older, we moved sections of sprinklers across acres of alfalfa and cut and baled hay. On weekends we ground our own livestock feed—wheat and milo with some alfalfa—the dustiest, loudest work on the farm. As hard as the work was, it was nice that we could pick some of our chores. Dwight liked the mechanical side of farming and ranching. I preferred the animals. But no matter what we chose, we each had about two solid hours of chores a day.

My parents made sure we had time for fun too. Dwight and I explored. We dug for imaginary pirate treasure. We searched for magpie nests among the upper tree branches to see what the birds had collected. We built forts between the juniper tree trunks, made mud pies, exploded dirt clods against the barn wall, and threw pitchforks into the haystack. Catching critters was our favorite pursuit.

Dwight and I played constantly—and we fought constantly. We had opposite personalities and often approached tasks in opposite ways, whether we were draining the sprinkler pipes or corralling the horses. I wanted to catch animals; Dwight wanted to let them go. He liked speed; I wanted to take my time. Many times our disagreements turned into an all-out war. We threw dirt or rocks at each other and sometimes swung fists. But our arguments never kept us apart for long.

Every Thursday Mom baked eight loaves of white bread: one for each day of the week and one to be eaten right out of the oven, dripping with homemade honey butter. That was our favorite treat, far better than the "snacks" Dwight and I would pilfer from the barrel full of dog food in the well house. We were never starving, of course, but we liked to pretend we were shipwrecked and needed any kind of food to survive. The nuggets of dog food gave us a sense of independence and also helped keep our German shepherd, Lady, close by on our adventures. I'll admit, we tried a few bites as we wandered the woods of Florida Mesa. (At least we knew if we were ever lost in the wilderness, we wouldn't die of hunger.)

Our family moved a few times. When I was in fourth grade, Mom and Dad took us to Bayfield, another nearby ranching town. They'd bought a sow pig with piglets and joined a hog cooperative, which held the promise of more cash. Though Dad still drove a grader in the Durango area, he and Mom worked from dawn to dusk around the seventeen-acre farm. For the first three months, we lived in a camper while we repaired the house on the property to make it livable. Life in the camper thrilled me. We kids would eat and then scatter outside until time for the next meal.

The property was a kid's paradise. We had a frog pond that fed into a larger pond. The big pond had been stocked years earlier with brown and rainbow trout, but it hadn't been fished. Apple trees lined the pond's west side, and a small dock was at the south end. Dad built a raft for us out of barrels and planks. He attached it by a rope to the dock so we could fish from it or, when the weather grew warm, splash around in the water. There were

The property was a kid's paradise.

endless tadpoles to raise, acres to roam, and all the apples we could eat. We lost interest in the dog food.

Just one year later, Dad received an offer to partner with a cousin on a pig farm and cattle ranch in Tularosa, New Mexico, about four hundred miles away. It was Dad's dream to ranch full-time, so we moved again. Our new farm had a brick house, a barn for milk cows, a hay barn, an equipment barn, a farrowing house where sows would give birth to piglets, and various corrals for calves and horses. Around us, the landscape was flat, with mesquite bushes and sandy soil. When the wind blew, which was often, the sand piled around the mesquite bushes, creating big mounds of sand and thorns.

Our house was isolated. We had no close neighbors, no television, no computer, not even a phone. But I loved this new chapter of life with Mom and Dad both working at home.

In that arid land, where heat waves blurred the horizon, each of us kids got a pony. A brown and white pony was loitering in our alfalfa field when we moved in. We named him Brighty, and he became Sandra's. Mine was a paint-Shetland mix we called Little Boy. Dwight's pony was a gray dapple named Maggie.

For fun and adventure, Dwight and I would ride for miles around our land. It seldom rained in southern New Mexico in the summer, but when it did, it was often a downpour: sheets of water, thunder, and lightning. After the lightning passed, we'd climb on our horses and go exploring. Rain would flood the hard-packed earth, causing animals to pop out of their burrows in search of higher ground. Rabbits. Coyotes. Rattlesnakes. Tarantulas. Bobcats. Ground squirrels. It was like riding through a desert zoo. When it snowed, we'd follow animal tracks to discover their homes.

Sandra sometimes came on rides with us, but she never liked to go far. Her pony knew the way home. So whenever she was finished exploring, Sandra simply turned around, and Brighty would take her back.

It seemed new babies were constantly born on the place. There were piglets, calves, and chicks everywhere. So we should have realized what was happening when Mom started looking bigger and skinnier at the same time. Dwight, Sandra, and I drew straws to see who would ask Mom about her oddly increasing size. I drew the short straw. One morning before church, I made my way to her bedroom and complimented her on her hair and dress. Then I took a deep breath and mentioned she seemed to be growing. She just chuckled. That was in 1972, when I was eleven. A month later, our little brother, D'Shane, was born.

> Our parents treated all of us alike, with respect, responsibility, and freedom.

Our childhood home was full of love. Our parents treated all of us alike, with respect, responsibility, and freedom. No one was a second-class citizen.

But school was an entirely different world.

SCHOOL WOES

As early as first grade, I began to have stomachaches and feel dizzy when it was time to take tests at school. Something as common as a spelling test could bring on such anxious symptoms, and they wouldn't fade. In the following years, school remained a challenge and a source of stress.

My parents took me to a doctor. "She's just spoiled, with a nervous disposition," the physician told them. He recommended a prescription tranquilizer that would calm me when I got anxious. But Mom and Dad did not fill that prescription. They were too wise, and besides, they couldn't afford it. Instead, they helped me in their own way. Whenever they saw my anxiety raising its head, my parents put me to work. "Tammie Jo," Dad would say, "I really need your help in the barn today. You can catch up with school tomorrow."

Looking back, I have no doubt that medicine would have ruined my life. It would have disqualified me from flying, and more, in the future. I'm grateful for my parents' wisdom and determination to keep life real for me. Obviously this doctor didn't know me, and his perception that I was spoiled affected his medical advice.

Putting my body in motion was what I needed to keep my mind clear. The physical work always calmed me and improved my attitude. How big was my trouble after all? My mom had a mantra: "No matter what, the sun will rise, and the birds will sing." Life would go on; the work would get done; the problems would pass. The following day, I would go back to school and face whatever it was that had me worked up—only then I was ready to face it.

Some of my schools were tough. The fourth-grade fashion police were appalled by my crime of wearing a skirt every other day. This was my mom's rule: "If you're a girl," she would say, "you should look like one." If I wore pants one day, I had to wear a dress the next. I didn't mind. Well, I didn't mind too much. I was never a tomboy, but clothes weren't going to limit me at recess. No matter what I wore, I could play kickball or climb a tree. However, my skirts didn't win me any friends.

Not fitting in at school made it harder to care about

getting good grades. When my parents realized this, they promised Dwight and me that if we made all As and Bs, we'd each get our own .22 gauge rifle. This was all the motivation we needed. Dwight hit the mark, I came close, and they kept their promise.

Giving rifles to kids may seem shocking today, but it made perfect sense for a farm family in the 1970s. Shooting was part of growing up for my parents, and they made it part of our journey through childhood. It was a skill we needed to defend our animals against predators. There were always skunks trying to get into the chicken coop and foxes trying to steal our rabbits. Dad taught us how to handle a gun safely before we earned the right to shoot it; then he taught us how to aim and hit a target. We weren't allowed to use our rifles unless Mom or Dad was with us. Getting the rifle reminded me that my parents held me to the same standard they held my older brother to, with the same reward.

Sandra also faced difficulties in school. Sandra had the most beautiful honey-brown hair, brown eyes, and fair skin. Small for her age, Sandra was quick-witted, with a cute little sense of humor and a ready smile. But kids paid more attention to her cerebral palsy, which gave her a limp and a crossed eye. She had to walk with her head tilted in an unusual way so she could see the ground ahead.

Sandra struggled to learn how to read and write, and numbers meant nothing to her. Teachers sometimes called her horrible names: slow, stupid, defiant. They thought she was being a troublemaker when she got up in class, walked forward, then stopped and stared at the blackboard. Why didn't they understand she was only trying to figure out what had been written there? At the time, public schools weren't as prepared as they are now to teach kids with disabilities. Mom and Dad were overworked, and they couldn't afford a private school. And as far as my parents knew, homeschooling didn't exist. So Sandra bravely struggled on, and we all did the best we could to protect her and help her with her schoolwork.

All of these challenges, plus the hard work of ranching, started to build my confidence and forced me to be tough. I discovered I had some strengths and could bounce back from difficult situations.

One of the things I did to relax was ride out into the middle of nowhere. I saved my money and bought a beautiful but small sorrel horse named Peanuts. Peanuts was a wonderful horse, high-spirited but trustworthy. Whenever I bridled Peanuts for a ride, Rascal, another German shepherd, would get so excited he would run circles around us. They both loved chasing rabbits.

> All of these challenges . . . forced me to be tough.

One day when I was riding, Peanuts and Rascal spotted a jackrabbit at the same time. Peanuts bolted after the rabbit with Rascal close behind.

Galloping without any fences in sight can be thrilling, so I tightened my grip on the reins. I let Peanuts run as fast as he wished and enjoyed the wind tearing through my hair. My horse seemed to be running at the speed of light. But he wasn't out of control—at first. I think he just loved the thrill of the run. I did too.

Soon the rabbit disappeared, and Rascal and Peanuts shifted from chasing to racing . . . each other! Peanuts wouldn't slow. I pulled on one rein to swing him into a tight circle. He went even faster. Directly ahead was a twelve-foot, sand-covered mesquite bush dotted with inch-long thorns. Peanuts was charting a course straight into the thorny mound, with me on his back. No matter what I tried, he held his speed.

My heart pounded as I realized my option to jump off had already passed. I didn't panic, but I knew this was going to hurt. I took my feet out of the stirrups and tried to shift myself sideways.

Peanuts hit the mesquite and flipped tail over head, with me tumbling underneath him. I hit the ground hard.

When the dust cleared, I saw Peanuts far in the distance. He had somehow somersaulted over me, righted himself, and kept running. I'd narrowly missed being smashed flat. It was a good thing, because the horse weighed about eight hundred pounds—heavy enough to have done real damage if he had landed on me.

Though I was scratched, bloody, and bruised, no bones were broken. Rascal gave up the race and returned to lick my cheek. We headed home, about a mile away, on foot. When I got there, Dad simply commented that I might be getting too big for Peanuts.

Things got better for a while after we moved to New Mexico. My fifth-grade class was a friendly group, happy to welcome a new face. Amazingly, we all got along. We were diverse, mostly Hispanic, Apache Indian, and white. But we didn't pay much attention to race, skin color, or gender. All that mattered to us was whether we had enough people to form softball or kickball teams during recess. Could you hit, catch, and throw? That was the only real question we had for one another.

During an interschool track meet, different homerooms competed against each other. When it came to the relay races, I got drafted to run on the boys' team. Our team won, and we each got a blue ribbon. I don't remember it being a big deal. But the experience stuck with me. If I wanted to do something (like run) and had what it took to do it well, then I would be welcome to do it.

Or so I thought.

BIG-SKY DREAMS

In the endless blue sky that hung over our New Mexico ranch, pilots from Holloman Air Force Base practiced dogfighting almost daily. They climbed and dived, chasing each other in practice battles. These pilots trained in T-38s—sleek white jets with tiny wings and pointy noses. I watched them in awe, my mouth wide open.

When pilots are dogfighting, they need a reference point on the ground to keep track of their location. The Air Force pilots used our three-story hay barn for this. The noise from the jets would start as a distant rumble as they approached our ranch. The roar would build, and sometimes it ended with the crack of a sonic boom, which meant the jets were flying fast enough to break the sound barrier.

On a few occasions, these booms broke windows in our barn. One night we heard an extra-loud crack, and in the morning we found one of our corrals laid flat. The steers penned inside had been so spooked by the noise that they busted out and ran a mile down the road. In spite of these bothers, Dad never said a harsh word when the noise of those jets caused the ground to shake. He would smile and say, "The sound of freedom."

Late one afternoon when I was in junior high school, I helped Mom in the garden. She devoted an entire acre to vegetables, and once the harvest began, she would be canning the rest of the summer. We pulled up beets and weeded around green beans. She replanted radishes while I replanted carrots.

Heat rippled off the desert floor. From time to time we both stole glances upward at the jets chasing each other across the sky. They raced straight up, twirling and hanging in space, then pointed their noses downward, accelerating toward the ground only to loop around and soar again into the sky.

"That's what I want to do," I said to my mom. With her hazel eyes and curled dark hair, she was striking even when she was working in the garden. She wiped the sweat from her brow and shook her head.

"Tammie Jo, those people are smart." She motioned toward the sky. "Besides, you can't fly. You have cavities."

Cavities? What on earth did teeth have to do with flying? As I pondered this surprising problem, she returned to pulling weeds. I was a good student, so I knew Mom didn't mean I wasn't smart. She was only saying that military flight school was demanding. To me that was no problem. I was happy to study as much as I needed to.

My parents never told me that I could do *anything* I wanted to do in life. They were too sensible to say something that would ring so hollow.

Once I told my mom my dream of becoming a racehorse jockey. Without hesitation she said, "No, Tammie Jo. You're five foot seven and growing. You're too tall to be a jockey. Move on to something *you* can do. Jockeying is not it." Even then I saw the wisdom in her words. Horse jockeys are shorter than five seven to stay below the weight limits.

I casually brought up my question about cavities and flying a few days later as our family sat around the dinner table. It came out that Mom thought cavities could explode at high altitudes (which I soon learned wasn't true). She gave a shrug and sent my question to Dad.

Dad set down his fork and took a long sip of his coffee, bypassing the cavity issue as if he understood my greater, unspoken question: *Can I become a pilot?*

Dad looked at me and said, "Well, find a pilot to talk to." Then he told me of his time in the Army and later the Air Force during the Korean War. He had served as a truck mechanic.

I nodded and grinned inside as I finished eating my dinner. *Okay then,* I thought. *It's not a no.*

After that, flying consumed my thoughts. I couldn't shake loose from the idea of becoming a pilot. I would do this. I would fly airplanes. I just needed a chance.

In addition to spending as much time as I could outdoors, I fed my hungry mind with books. At first Dwight and I were hooked on mysteries, and Edgar Rice Burroughs gave us our superhero, Tarzan. When I read *A Princess of Mars*, another Burroughs book, I found a heroine I could really cheer for too. Dejah Thoris was fierce in her protection of her people and willing to do daring things to stand up for them.

Flying consumed my thoughts.

I also read the Bible because I found it exciting. I read it for the heroes, the romance, and the battles. I discovered a wealth of strong and fearless leaders: Moses, Daniel, and Joseph. There were heroines as well. I read of Deborah, a prophetess who helped lead her people in battle, and of Queen Esther, who stepped between disaster and her Jewish people. I also loved the story of Ruth the Moabite who quietly and selflessly braved hardship to take care of her mother-in-law.

Books were the keyhole I could peer through into worlds other than my own. I read the classic horse books: *Black Beauty, The Black Stallion, The Horse and His Boy.* Soon enough, I turned to aviation literature. I read about Amelia Earhart and other early lady pioneers in flight, such as Beryl Markham. Markham was the first person to fly solo, nonstop, east to west across the Atlantic—that is, *into the wind.*

Then one summer, I read *Jungle Pilot*, a biography about missionary pilot Nate Saint. A patriotic kid who longed to fly, Saint joined the US Army Air Corps during World War II. Nate was disqualified from flying for medical reasons, so he became an Army aircraft mechanic. After the war, he became a private pilot who flew food and medicine to people in remote villages of Ecuador. I read and reread *Jungle Pilot*, soaking up Nate's story.

Nate Saint had loved his country, and he'd longed to fly. In that, we were the same. I considered joining the military as he had. If I did that, I could both serve my country and fly. *Okay then*, I thought. *I know exactly what I want to do.* I just needed to grow up and set my plans in motion.

At the time, it all seemed easy enough.

WHAT IS DOGFIGHTING?

Dogfighting is the informal term for aerial combat maneuvers (ACM). In dogfighting, one aircraft tries to get in a position behind another aircraft, close enough to shoot it down with guns or missiles. Fighter pilots dogfight to defend an area, ships, or themselves from an enemy aircraft that has managed to get in close. Dogfighting is becoming a dying form of battle as weapons become more advanced (such as missiles that can travel longer ranges), but pilots still learn the skill.

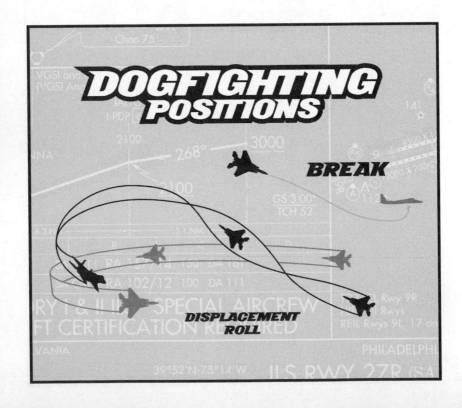

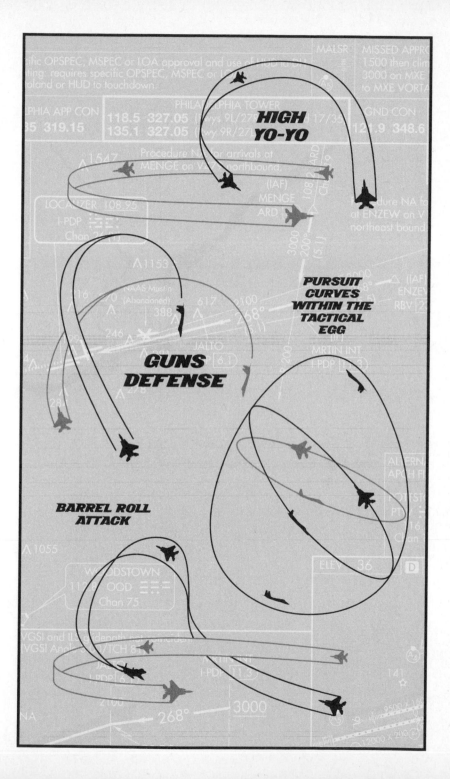

THIEVES AND BULLIES

When I was in middle school, our hogs started disappearing from their pens. We counted every animal when they were fed morning and night, so we knew we were dealing with thieves.

One night Dwight received an award at school, and Mom and Dad attended the assembly with him. I was about twelve, just old enough to babysit Sandra and baby D'Shane. Before they left, my parents turned on all the lights to discourage the thieves from striking while they were gone.

Soon after dark, a truck slowly idled past our house. Then it slowed down further as it came close to the pig-pens. *The hog thieves,* I thought, and I quickly made a plan. For most of my childhood we didn't have a phone, so I didn't think of calling anyone for help. I turned off all the lights in the house, explained my plan to Sandra, and told her to watch D'Shane.

Not long afterward the truck came by again, more slowly this time. Staying out of sight, I crept out our front door and made my way through the cattle corrals toward the pigpens. I watched as the truck turned again and slowly drove back toward our house for the third time. Then it pulled up alongside the barbed-wire fence and parked. Two figures emerged from the truck and softly closed the doors. They hopped the fence and headed for the closest pen of pigs. I felt sad when I recognized them. They were two of our hired hands.

All at once, I ran toward them through a corral full of Brangus calves, waving my hands and screaming, "Get out of here!" The cattle spooked. They crisscrossed the corral snorting, braying, and kicking.

With all the commotion, the thieves abandoned their plans and bounded back over the barbed-wire fence. One of them ripped his pants and cursed. The truck doors slammed, the engine roared to life, and they sped away.

When my parents came home, I told them the news. They were doubly stunned that I'd confronted the thieves and that the young men were people we'd trusted. The next day Dad fired them.

Losing a few hogs was nothing compared to the loss

of the ranch when my father's ranching partnership collapsed suddenly. We lost everything but one old car and ten pigs. Our family stayed in the area but moved to a smaller property.

During those difficult years, I was lucky to make some great friends in middle school. None of them were too stressed about being popular. It just wasn't that important to them. So I was surprised when the coolest group of girls on the planet invited me to hang out with them. I tried not to act as shocked as I felt, and my friends encouraged me to join the group. They agreed that the invitation was, by junior high standards, a life-changing opportunity. I'd just won the popularity lottery!

I didn't hold on to my new status for long, though. Hanging out with cool kids was awkward for me. I didn't belong. They weren't interested in anything I had to say. After a few days, the girls told me to go away. They said I was too tall and made them look weird.

My star rose and fell in less than a week. It was a school-wide scandal. Hurt and embarrassed, I tried to hide. I couldn't look my old, sweet friends in the eye, so I looked for a quiet place to eat my lunch alone. I went behind the sprawling firethorn bushes that grew along the front of the school building, thinking I could eat alone and disappear—at least for lunch hour.

To my surprise, I wasn't the only kid there. A host of misfits ate lunch behind those bushes: the loners, the shy kids, the poorly dressed boys, the pimply faced girls. We were all just struggling to make it on the playground of life. The hangout was simply called "behind the bushes," and anyone who had a hard time fitting in was welcome there. This sheltered spot became a regular retreat for me.

Behind the bushes, our masks were down. We could talk to each other without worrying about being made fun of. Many of the kids there were smart and witty and funny, even wise. We helped each other with our homework. We shared laughs and listened to each other's stories. I rejoined my loyal friends after a while, but I made lasting friendships behind the bushes. The kids there taught me how complex and wonderful different kinds of friendships can be.

I never wanted to be in a cool group again.

During my middle school years, Sandra was in elementary school. We rode the same bus to and from school because the buildings were across the street from one another. After school, one mean kid sometimes got to the bus stop before I did, and he made Sandra his special target. Walking never came easy for

I never wanted to be in a cool group again.

Sandra, and this bully thought it was funny to trip her as she climbed the bus steps. Or he'd bump her before she got on and send her sprawling on the sidewalk. Humiliated and dirty, she'd struggle to get back up. He wasn't the only bully who ever tormented Sandra, but he was one of the most predictable.

One night our family sat around the supper table and talked about bullying. My folks reminded us that bullies are seldom cruel to just one person. When you stand up to a bully, you're helping not only one person but the many others in the bully's path. They also said that silence is consent. If you see injustice but don't do something about it, then you're part of the problem. The right not to be bullied is a pretty basic one for anyone.

Two days later, the bully was at it again. As I approached the bus stop at the end of the school day, I saw him shove Sandra under the parked bus. Then he laughed at her and called her an idiot. I ran to Sandra and helped her get up. I dusted her off, gave her a hug, and dried her tears. She cared about her clothes, and now her dress was filthy. And one of her knees had been scraped up. I knew she felt humiliated.

"Don't worry about it," I whispered to her. "Small people have small ways. I promise you—he will *never* do this again."

Startled, Sandra looked into my eyes. She held my gaze a moment, then looked away. "Okay," she said. Her voice was small.

By now the bully was on the bus, sneering and bragging to his friends about his mighty deed.

I helped Sandra climb aboard. After I got her into a seat near the front, I walked straight back to the bully and took care of him myself.

I told him, "Never. Ever. Do that again." I made sure my instructions were as loud as his mocking had been.

The bully and his friends were shocked into silence. His game was over, and he knew it. The bus driver never said a word, but our eyes met in the big rearview mirror mounted above his head, and I saw a little grin tug at the corners of his mouth.

There are times when we simply have to stand between someone else and harm.

My mom made sure we went to church as a family. My dad thought the hours spent there could have been spent more productively on the land, but Mom insisted that church was important, and Dad didn't argue. So every Sunday we drove from Tularosa to the bigger town of Alamogordo to attend a Nazarene fellowship.

I loved church because it was fun. As teenagers, Dwight and I lobbied to attend Sunday evening services as well. That was when we could actually visit and chat with our friends—during choir practice, probably too much during the service, then during youth group afterward.

In the summer, the pastor crafted sandboards for the teenagers so we could surf the dunes at nearby White Sands National Monument. In the winter, he took us inner-tubing up in the snow of the mountains. Throughout the year, the church teens gathered at the city park for brownies and lemonade. We played flag football and Frisbee, sang songs, and listened to short devotionals that we took turns writing ourselves.

The summer before I started high school, Dwight and I attended church camp for the first time. Mom convinced Dad to let us off work for the entire week, so we left the heat of the ranch behind us and headed to the campground in the mountains.

Each morning after breakfast, we went to a chapel session with skits and songs, followed by an interesting speaker who knew how to capture teenagers' attention. After lunch, we played field sports and competed in everything from scavenger hunts to a teenage version of red rover, in which both teams crossed the field simultaneously, trying not to get tackled. There were always a few kids who had to go see the nurse following that game. After dinner we sat around a campfire on rock-tiered seats in a three-quarter amphitheater. We performed skits, told funny stories, and heard encouraging messages that made us realize we were all walking a similar road. We sang songs about God without anything but crickets and the local whip-poor-wills to accompany us. Camp was an absolute oasis.

Because I grew up outside, I saw sunrises and sunsets as I went about my chores and adventures. If the *Farmer's Almanac* predicted an early moonrise, I would make sure I watched it from my favorite spot: a big square post a half mile away from the house and barn, near a small pond.

I would watch as daytime sights and sounds turned to nighttime. The sun would set over the western mountains, the San Andres, and the moon would rise over the eastern mountains, the Sacramentos.

This time of wonder in the everyday scenes of nature sent me on a search. I wanted to know who thought this up and had the chemistry set to make it work! I compared what I heard at school with what I heard at home and what I read about other cultures. It seemed everyone had a story about our beginnings, and each story required a certain element of faith. I settled on the "beginning story" told in the Bible because it made sense to me. Now, years later at camp, I realized God was more than a Creator.

That year when I was twelve, I had a big shift in my thinking about God. My image of God had been that of an angry, bearded old man in the sky waiting for me to mess up. Now I realized that wasn't Him at all. My experience at camp replaced that image with one of a young man who walked the same earth I was walking. By the time camp was over, I had come to see God as an ally, someone who loves me. He wasn't asking me to behave. He was asking me to believe one simple truth: He loves me. This was a major turning point in my life. I didn't find religion. I found a relationship with a God who was wise and wanted the best for me. This has been the way I have thought about my faith throughout my life.

When Dwight and I came home from camp, we compared notes. He had made the same decision I had, to believe God loved him. Mom and Dad noticed we didn't argue hourly, and when we did disagree, we settled it with words and not with fists. We were kinder and more patient with each other. Decisions have consequences, and this decision brought peace to our family life.

CAREER DAY

I did my best thinking outside. I loved the wide New Mexico countryside and the wind blowing across my face. But at times I felt anxious. My entry into high school was difficult. Sandra's bully-on-the-bus had a bully big sister who did her best to intimidate and threaten me. Because I stood much taller than most of my classmates, even as a freshman, I had no hope of going unnoticed.

Once again, outdoor adventures calmed my heart— and my nerves. Whenever I felt frustrated or angry, I went outside and found something to do. I liked to do wood- working projects, and Dad had shown me how to use the power tools. There was always a pile of wood scraps to choose from. I would build a frame, whittle a spoon, or make a guitar for Sandra or D'Shane, and my thoughts would settle down.

By that time in life, I was devoted to journaling. I had been helping my dad with the ranch journal, and I started keeping my own when I bought my first calf. The ranch journal had hay and grain yields and prices as well as cattle and hog births and sales. My journal was all about my Brangus steer, George. In the beginning, I carefully noted his growth and feed costs. Within weeks, however, my entries started to wander away from farming facts. I wrote poems, prayers, ideas, memories of activities with my friends, stories of life around the farm, and thoughts about God.

After I decided to believe that God loves me, I started reading my Bible every morning. Now I saw that it was a love story, not a book of rules. I found courage in its pages. I realized God had put it in me to be wise and strong.

At school, the bully and her group hung out in the school bathroom, so I avoided it. The locker hallway might have been another dangerous place for me, but I received a locker among the senior boys. I was embarrassed to be among them at first, but the school secretary refused to change my locker assignment. To my surprise, these guys I didn't know wound up being my protectors.

In time I came out of my shell. I ran track, played flute, and cheered on the cheerleading squad. I sang in plays, studied hard, passed silly notes in class, and led the student council my senior year. I had plenty to keep me busy.

My junior year, I boarded an airplane for the first time. I'd signed up for a school trip to Washington, DC, and was excited but scared. The evening before we left, I quietly said goodbye to every horse, cow, hog, and dog on our farm, just in case this was the last time I would ever see them.

On October 31, 1977, I boarded the plane, found my seat, and buckled in. When the flight attendant stood to give her safety talk, I listened hard, desperate to remember everything. Then the plane powered up and began moving. We accelerated slowly at first, then more quickly, until we were hurtling down the runway faster than anything I'd ever imagined. Then came the liftoff. The whole plane felt weightless.

I had imagined what it would be like to fly, but I wasn't prepared for the sensation of motionlessness once we arrived above the clouds. It seemed we stood still as the world turned beneath us.

Later that night I wrote in my journal: *This flying business is really something else! It's as if I'm in another world, land, even existence.*

On the plane there were *nine* radio channels. That really impressed me as a kid who had only a tape player and a radio at home! Who knew so much entertainment could be found on one airplane? As fantastic as it was, the lineup didn't excite me as much as the view from the window. Looking down on the clouds

> Looking down on the clouds thrilled me.

thrilled me. We were actually hanging there, suspended in air. Airborne.

My senior year, I climbed aboard a big yellow school bus and headed to the high school in Alamogordo for a career day program. I had signed up for an aviation class with an Air Force pilot. My heart leaped at the chance to participate.

Our bus arrived late, and all my friends scattered to their own interests. It took me some time before I finally found the classroom where the lecture on aviation was underway. The door creaked as I entered the room packed with boys. The Air Force pilot, a colonel, was speaking up front. He stood tall at the blackboard. The colonel stopped talking and stared at me. Every head turned in my direction.

"Are you lost?" the colonel asked.

"Um . . . no, sir," I said. "I signed up for aviation."

His voice was flat. "Well, girls don't fly for a living, and this is career day, not hobby day. You might want to find something you can do."

I felt as if I'd been smacked.

I sat down in the nearest open seat, too embarrassed to leave. The buses were locked. Where else could I go? Besides, I wanted to hear the lecture.

The colonel ignored me and went on. For a while I forgot his rebuke and listened. His descriptions of aviation sounded fabulous! Flying was both mentally and physically challenging, he explained. In Air Force training, after you master flying one airplane, you move up to a faster, more complicated one. He described the different places around the world you could fly, the missions, and the community. The Air Force sounded like the perfect place to serve my country and be a pilot.

Later, I learned that women had been allowed into the Air Force's flight training school for three years at the time the colonel dismissed me. The colonel would have known this. Why he told me otherwise, I will never know.

Back at my high school in Tularosa, I stepped off the bus and headed straight for the guidance counselor's office. But she sided with the colonel and told me to find another line of work. My aviation dreams were dashed. I couldn't afford to fly as a hobby. I needed a profession, a way to earn a living.

That night Rascal and I sat together on top of a hay-stack, where I could see the stars and breathe deeply of the alfalfa's clean, rich, earthy smell. I told my dog the disappointing news. He was unfazed.

More than once my mother had calmed my fears about my future. "God purposely created you," she would say. "There's a reason you're drawn to certain things. Find what you're drawn to *and* what you're well suited for—then go do it!"

In the crisp night air, with Mom's wisdom in mind, I formed a new plan. I wasn't as excited about this one as I had been about flying, but it seemed interesting and practical. I'd always enjoyed working with the animals around our farm. For years I'd helped birth calves and pigs. I'd vaccinated, dehorned, and stitched up livestock, and I'd bottle-fed and medicated just about every kind of animal. I was good at it. I would still go to college, I decided. But I would study to become a veterinarian.

That year in my English class, I decided to memorize a stanza from a poem called "To a Waterfowl":

> He, who, from zone to zone,
> Guides through the boundless sky thy certain
>   flight,
> In the long way that I must trace alone,
> Will lead my steps aright.

The poet, William Cullen Bryant, had written those words during his own struggle to decide his future. Maybe my first dream had been sidelined, but I wasn't going to pout my life away. There would be another adventure out there with my name on it.

WOMEN WITH WINGS

Women have been pilots of one kind or another since humans first learned to fly. During World War II, women all over the world flew for their nation's militaries. Russia formed three combat squadrons of women: a fighter squadron, a night bombing squadron, and a day bombing squadron. *Night Witches* is a short and interesting book about them.

However in most countries, women pilots weren't considered soldiers, and they weren't allowed to fly in combat. In the United States, the Navy was the first of the armed services to open flight training to women, in 1973. The Army followed in 1974 (when they opened helicopter training to female pilots). And the Air Force followed in 1976. Some people stayed unhappy about this change for a long time. When the Air Force colonel told Tammie Jo that "girls don't fly for a living," it was 1979.

WOMEN PILOTS
IN THE
US MILITARY

WORLD WAR II

★ **1942** WOMEN PILOTS FLY MILITARY AIRCRAFT FOR THE FIRST TIME.

★ **1943** WOMEN AIRFORCE SERVICE PILOTS (WASP) IS ESTABLISHED.

★ **WOMEN AVIATORS** SERVE AS
- test pilots
- flight instructors
- cargo deliverers
- ferry pilots to deliver new planes from factories
- flying chauffeurs for leaders
- tow plane pilots, dragging targets for ground and aerial gunnery training

★ **ALL PILOTS TRAIN** IN
- Morse code
- meteorology
- military law
- physics
- aircraft mechanics
- navigation

★ ABOUT **1,000** WOMEN FLY MORE THAN **60 MILLION** MILES. **38** DIE WHILE SERVING.

★ **1977** CONGRESS GRANTS WWII FEMALE PILOTS VETERAN STATUS.

AFTER WWII, WOMEN ARE **NOT ALLOWED** TO BE MILITARY PILOTS **UNTIL THE 1970s.**
- **1973** Navy
- **1974** Army and Coast Guard
- **1976** Air Force

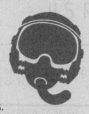

★ **1975** ROSEMARY CONATSER (LATER MARINER) PILOTS A FIGHTER JET.

★ **1986** A FEMALE NAVY OFFICER BECOMES A JET TEST PILOT.

★ **1990** CDR. ROSEMARY MARINER COMMANDS A 300-MEMBER SQUADRON OF NAVY JET PILOTS.

★ **1991** TAMMIE JO SHULTS, PAM LYONS, AND LORI MELLING TRAIN IN F/A-18 HORNETS.

★ **1993** THE MILITARY ALLOWS WOMEN TO FLY COMBAT MISSIONS.

★ **1995** PAM LYONS FLIES THE F/A-18 HORNET IN COMBAT.

★ **6.5%** OF MILITARY PILOTS ARE WOMEN.

★ **7%** OF NON-MILITARY PILOTS ARE WOMEN.

★ TODAY, WOMEN PILOTS IN THE MILITARY HAVE THE **SAME JOBS** AS MEN.

· fighter pilots
· bomber pilots
· navigators
· tanker pilots
· weapons officers
· loadmasters

GUYS AND GIRLS

My plan to become a veterinarian fell apart as fast as my hopes of becoming a pilot.

Dwight and I were the first in our family to attend college, and we understood that everyone would have to take on extra work to pay for our education. Farms can make a lot of food, but they rarely make a lot of money.

Dwight waited a year for me to graduate so we could start college at the same time. Both of us were accepted to MidAmerica Nazarene College in Kansas, and our family made the trip there an adventure. We'd been on only one vacation during our childhood, so the trip was exciting. I loved the beautiful change of scenery, shifting from Southwestern deserts and mountains to rolling Midwestern fields bursting with crops.

It was 1979, and at eighteen and seventeen years old, Dwight and I were excited about the future.

When school started, I got work at fast-food restaurants. Each morning I made biscuits at Hardee's. Each evening I sold roast beef sandwiches and french fries at Arby's. I told myself I didn't have time for friends, but in truth I was lonely and homesick. Dwight and I tried to meet every day for lunch. But with different schedules and only a hallway phone in each of our dorms, even that much contact was hard to coordinate. My parents didn't have phone service on our remote farm, so we would write them letters to plan times when they could be at either a pay phone in Tularosa or at our uncle's tire shop in Alamogordo.

Things got a little better when a girl in my dorm talked me into trying out for the track team. All those years of bucking hay bales and throwing hatchets and pitchforks had built up my arm strength. I earned a spot on the team for the 400-meter run and three field events: discus (hurling a four-pound disc), shot put (push-throwing a heavy ball), and javelin (throwing a spear). Javelin was new to me and quickly became my favorite. Track came with a small scholarship, which helped pay for my books.

I made the volleyball team next and cut back my hours making biscuits and selling sandwiches. More importantly, I spent more time outside and around people—nice people, who quickly became my family away from home.

Over the next four years, I threw myself into sports and studies. I went out for cheerleading and was elected captain of the squad. I became vice president of the agriculture club and a senior homecoming princess. My senior year, I earned an All-American title in javelin by placing first at a national track meet.

Things were less rosy at home, however. My parents worked every day from sunup until sundown, but money was always in short supply. In the early 1980s, the prices of beef cattle and hogs were low, and it became harder to make a living as a farmer or rancher. Both of my parents took extra work outside the farm.

Once when I visited home during my junior year, my little brother, D'Shane, said at the dinner table, "Tammie Jo, I love it when you come home." My heart warmed. "When you're here, we eat meat," he added.

Mom and Dad exchanged glances. They hadn't wanted me to know they'd stopped spending money on meat and saved all of our livestock to sell. They were living on baked potatoes out of the garden.

My heroic parents were determined to help me get an education. But as I approached graduation, I realized that in spite of all their efforts, vet school was just too expensive. With my sports scholarships ending and student loans mounting, I needed to be honest with myself. It was time to get serious about life after college. What would I do for *work*?

In the fall of my senior year, the brother of my friend

Janice became an Air Force pilot, and the family invited me to go to the ceremony where he'd have his wings pinned to his uniform. I was happy to go, and I applauded with everybody else when he received his silver wings. But my mind was in another world.

Because there, right in front of me, sitting in the graduating class was . . . a girl. A female Air Force pilot!

My mind buzzed with excitement. This woman had made it! But how? *She must be some brilliant rocket scientist destined to become an astronaut*, I thought. Or maybe—just maybe—the military door wasn't as firmly shut to women as I had been told.

After the ceremony I made my way through the crowd to her. I introduced myself and asked how she'd done it. She explained she'd gone through her college's Reserve Officer Training Corps (ROTC) program. Because I was about to graduate, ROTC wasn't an option for me. Once again, my heart sank.

> There, right in front of me . . . was . . . a female Air Force pilot!

On our trip back to the college, my friend suggested that I get a *commission* as an officer and then apply to flight school. That night I could barely sleep, thinking about the possibilities.

Before I graduated, I visited an Air Force recruiting office and spoke to a *recruiter*. He said the Air Force wasn't interested in me. His answer was polite but firm.

I waited a while, then spoke with a different Air Force

recruiter. He was also polite and just as firm. No way, no how. It wasn't ever going to happen.

The Air Force was actively seeking pilots. I saw an ad in the newspaper encouraging people to apply. I clipped it out and took it with me when I made my third visit to the recruiting office.

This recruiter also shook his head. "If you have a brother with a degree who wants to be a pilot, bring him in," he said. "We aren't accepting applications from girls."

I heard the Army had pilots, so I spoke with them. They said I was not a fit and turned me away too.

Janice suggested I try the Navy. I didn't know much about the Navy. In my mind, the Navy had ships, and I wanted to fly. But Janice reminded me the Navy had aircraft carriers, which had jets.

The naval recruiter in Kansas was kinder than any recruiter I'd met. He invited me to take the Armed Services Vocational Aptitude Battery (ASVAB), an entrance exam that must be taken by everyone who wants to join any branch of the military. The test has about eight hundred questions that cover math, mechanics, electronics, science, and aviation aptitude. I took the test and missed passing by six questions. The recruiter told me that I could take the test again in six months, so I bought a book and started to study.

After graduating from college, I took the test again, this time in Texas, and passed. The recruiter there said, "Great job! You'll just need to come back when the officer recruiter can process your paperwork." He was all smiles.

I was so happy. I told my friends, "I'm in!"

I returned to have my paperwork processed. "We don't need girls," the officer told me. "I'm not processing your paperwork."

My brow furrowed. "But the other recruiter said I scored high enough," I said.

"You scored high enough for a guy," the man said, "but not for a girl."

I was heartbroken. How would I ever get past this guy/girl stuff? What did a girl have to do to serve her country as a pilot?

I didn't know what else to try. Once again, I cut the military out of my plans for the future.

WHAT IS ROTC?

ROTC stands for Reserve Officer Training Corps. It's a program at certain colleges (and some high schools) in the United States. In exchange for a scholarship, ROTC students, called *cadets*, study certain subjects and commit to serving the military as an officer for a certain number of years after they graduate. Four branches of the US military—the Army, Navy, Air Force, and Marine Corps—each have their own ROTC program. It's a relatively short-term commitment for a great opportunity.

ROTC

ROTC ALLOWS STUDENTS TO COMPLETE MILITARY OFFICER TRAINING WHILE EARNING A COLLEGE DEGREE.

- ★ 4 years
- ★ 1,700 US colleges

4 SERVICE BRANCHES

- ★ Army
- ★ Navy
- ★ Marine Corps
- ★ Air Force

CADETS RECEIVE

- ★ paid college education
- ★ books
- ★ room and board
- ★ money for monthly living costs
- ★ job after graduation

TRAINING INCLUDES

- ★ classes
- ★ hands-on field work
- ★ simulation exercises

CAREER OPTIONS INCLUDE

- ★ information technology (IT)
- ★ communications
- ★ engineering
- ★ business
- ★ education
- ★ law
- ★ health science
- ★ aviation
- ★ surface warfare

8 YEARS AVERAGE MILITARY SERVICE AFTER ROTC GRADUATION

- ★ 4 years active duty
- ★ 4 years in a reserve unit

ACTIVE-DUTY SERVICE MEMBERS RECEIVE

- ★ regular pay
- ★ healthcare
- ★ money for housing costs
- ★ paid vacation time
- ★ travel opportunities
- ★ retirement savings
- ★ ongoing education
- ★ career and leadership training

THE DREAM THAT WOULDN'T DIE

My parents had moved to Roswell, New Mexico—a town carved out of dirt and sand by wind—because Sandra needed to attend a specialized school located there. I didn't know what else to do with my life, so when I finished college, I packed up and went with them.

I got a job interview with a large agricultural company in Iowa. They offered to pay for a plane ticket for me, but I asked the hiring manager if I could have the money for an airplane rental and an instructor instead. To my surprise he said yes, so I found an instructor and rented a single-engine Cessna to take me to my interview.

It took quite a while to reach our destination in that small plane. On the way, the instructor talked to me about flying as I enjoyed the view from above the clouds—a little slower and a little lower than it had been on my trip to Washington, DC.

In Iowa, it turned out the job offer was to feed pigs. Pig farming is honest work. My dad had been a pig farmer, among other things, and I'd done that enough myself to be qualified. I said I'd consider it.

On the way home, the instructor stopped talking for a while. As we flew back over the great plains of Kansas, I felt the steady thrum of the engine matching my own breathing. By the time we glimpsed the majestic mountains east of Santa Fe, I knew I couldn't go back to feeding pigs. I would keep looking.

In Roswell I was a substitute teacher while I looked for a full-time job. Days of job searching turned into weeks. Then months. Then a year. I was a little surprised to discover that my dreams weren't going to take flight right away. In the meantime, I worked a couple of jobs and tried to be helpful at home. This wasn't what I had planned, but I enjoyed the time with my family.

> I felt the steady thrum of the engine matching my own breathing.

During that time, I signed up for flight lessons. Perhaps I was imagining that flying was better than it really was. I thought that if

I put in the hard work of actually learning to fly, it would help me let go.

On April 7, 1984, I drove out to Great Southwest Aviation, where Mr. Russ Reece gave me my first lesson. I loved it! Over the next few weeks, I took a couple more lessons. But one day as I drove home, I let some common sense settle in. I was the only person in my family with a college education. (Dwight had decided to return home after his first year at MidAmerica.) And I was the only one without a real job. An expensive hobby was the last thing on my list of to-dos in life. It was time to get real.

Mom saw how I enjoyed children and suggested I get my teaching credentials. The plan made sense. I took out more college loans and packed everything I owned into my old car. Then I drove to Silver City to begin graduate studies at Western New Mexico University.

Yet I still had a yearning deep in my heart. The desire to fly nagged me and wouldn't let go. But I couldn't complain. My life was going better. In addition to my graduate studies, I was busy with a job as a photographer for the university's alumni paper. So I changed my prayers. "Help me move on," I asked God. I prayed that prayer throughout my first semester of graduate school.

Yet the pull of flying didn't go away. It was even growing! Why could I not get past it?

I thought often about my mom's wisdom: *"God purposely created you. There's a reason you're drawn to certain things. Find what you're drawn to and what you're well suited for—then go do it!"*

My responsibility wasn't to worry about my future. It was to trust in God and work hard so that I would be ready when He sent opportunities my way. I decided to try the military one last time.

I called the Navy recruiter in Albuquerque because I'd be passing through that city on my way home for Christmas. He was new, and I'd never spoken with him before. I explained that I wanted to be a Navy pilot. I told him that I'd passed the ASVAB, and that I'd scored high enough for a guy, but not for a girl.

"Wait a minute," he said. "The Navy doesn't have different ASVAB requirements for men and women." He looked up my scores. "Your scores are terrific," he said. "Come by here before you head back to school in January. We'll get all your paperwork and application completed and turned in."

This recruiter kept his promise. One day in early January 1985, my application packet for the Navy was at last completed, submitted, and approved. I was accepted to Aviation Officer Candidate School! AOCS is a fourteen-week program in which college graduates can earn a naval commission without passing through the United States Naval Academy or ROTC. Every branch of the military has its own officer candidate school (OCS), but AOCS is the Navy's boot camp for those who want to fly.

Just two months later, I found myself in Pensacola, Florida, ready for my first step of a long march.

WHAT WERE YOU MADE TO DO?

Tammie Jo's mom often told her, "God purposely created you. There's a reason you're drawn to certain things. Find what you're drawn to *and* what you're well suited for—then go do it!"

How do you know what you're made for? Make three lists:

1. Things I love to do
2. Things I know or can learn
3. Things my body is suited for

What shows up on all three lists? If you try something new and it doesn't work out, don't be discouraged. By trying, you'll learn things that may turn out to be important later.

BOOT CAMP

The grounds of Naval Air Station Pensacola felt like a fancy college campus. Driving in, I viewed lawns that looked like golf-course greens, stretching between buildings smartly trimmed in white. I parked, shut the car door behind me, and gazed at the beautiful old red-brick buildings. Catty-corner across the street was a polished F-4 Phantom. The jet's nose was pointing right at the check-in building as if to say, "If you want to fly Navy, enter here." My pulse kicked up a notch as I hauled my luggage from the car and gathered my papers.

The building, I would soon learn, was called a battalion and was where the candidates lived. I walked up the steps and into the lobby. There, a group of men in khaki uniforms chatted with each other as they worked. One of them greeted me.

"Afternoon, ma'am. Help you find someone?"

"No, actually"—I held out my paperwork—"I'm here to check in."

My announcement caught the ears of the other men, and one of them shouted, "Secure your luggage to the—!" At the same time, another barked, "Bulkhead!" Soon all the men had joined in. They all shouted the same jumbled words: "Secure!" "Bulkhead!" "Luggage!" "Your!" I had no idea what it meant to secure something, and I was equally confused over the definition of a bulkhead.

When there was a lull in the shouting, I made the mistake of saying calmly, "If you would quit yelling, I could understand you." Their shouting only doubled in volume and confusion. "Your-to-luggage-bulkhead-secure!" Somehow I figured out that a bulkhead was a wall. Setting my luggage against the wall was my first order.

When my luggage was in its proper place, one of the khaki-clad men directed me by shouts to my room. It looked like a prison cell with its battleship-gray furniture, oversize metal lockers, and twin beds for four candidates. I soon learned there were about seventy-five candidates in our class, and only three of us were women. That was the highest number of women in an AOCS class to date. Much to the men's annoyance, class 1685 became known as the class of girls.

The next morning at 5:00 a.m., the whole class awoke

to the ear-splitting ruckus of metal trash cans careening down the hallway.

"Get up, you filthy maggots!" bellowed our drill instructor. The seniors in the program had warned us of this moment: When the drill instructor announced his arrival, we were to fall out into the hallway and stand at attention against the bulkhead. And we had better do it quickly.

I guess we weren't quick enough.

The drill instructor, Staff Sergeant Carney, informed us that we were the worst excuses for candidates he had ever seen. In his life. In the history of officer candidate school. Not only that, the way we were standing at attention was a disgrace to the United States Navy.

"On your face, maggots!" he ordered, and we dropped to a push-up position. We didn't do that right either, so we practiced a few dozen more times. He instructed us in the finer points of every exercise you can imagine: push-ups, leg lifts, jumping jacks, squat thrusts, lunges, and high-stepping. You name it, we did it.

"Get 'em!" was an order to begin the assigned exercise *right now*. For example, "Leg lifts, get 'em!" And we did leg lifts to the point of exhaustion. The whole routine was called PT, for physical training.

Staff Sergeant Carney was with the United States Marine Corps. He was fit, his uniform was crisp and spotless, and his expression was grim. He spoke perfectly clear English at the rate of a speeding freight train, insulting and demeaning us with a sharp wit.

He wanted us to do everything in a specific way. *His* way. That morning he explained his definition of *attention to detail*. Every day for the next three and a half months, we were trained to pay attention to every detail of everything we did. There was a proper way to stand at attention, to salute, to hold a fork, to do a push-up, to make a bed, to wear a uniform. There was even a proper way to lace up shoes. Every tiny issue mattered. At the time, I saw these demands as just another hurdle to clear to *become* a Navy pilot. I would later appreciate that attention to detail was an integral part of *being* a Navy pilot. Details can save your life.

"Class 1–6–8–5, meet me in the courtyard," Staff Sergeant Carney ordered. "And don't make me wait on you, ladies!"

> Details can save your life.

We all bolted to the courtyard. As I ran at full speed to get into formation, I passed behind the staff sergeant. He shouted, "Well, excuse me!"

Thinking he was being polite, I respectfully answered, "No, you're fine." Then I found my place in line and stood at attention.

Staff Sergeant Carney met me face-to-face and planted the brim of his campaign hat in the middle of my forehead. Scowling, he proceeded to explain, at the top of his lungs, that I should have said, "By your leave, sir," as I passed behind him. He used my "egregious display of disrespect" as an excuse to PT the whole class "until the cows came home." They didn't come home for a while that day.

When it was time for our military haircuts, we double-timed it to a nearby building. The staff sergeant shouted at us to line up. The men were placed first in line, arranged from tallest to shortest. The women were at the back, again tallest to shortest. My tall frame stood out at the short end of the lineup of men.

"You wreck the formation, Everest!" the drill instructor shouted at me.

Of course I did.

Inside the building, we fanned out into six lines facing six grinning barbers. Each buzzed away happily on the head of a new candidate. Three of the men in my battalion quit right there. After they were gone, candidate after candidate was shaved bald. The barbers were quick. Before I knew it, I had been sheared like a sheep. When I saw my shoulder-length hair on the floor, I simply thought, *Whatever.* It would grow back. And no way was I going to cry over lost hair, even if I did look like an alien.

We went straight from the barber to have our ID tags made. I mailed an extra picture home to my parents. Weeks later, when I was able to call home for the first time, Mom said to me, "Honey, please don't send any more photos until your hair grows out. You look like a prisoner of war. That picture scared your younger brother."

I didn't send any more pictures, but Mom sent

cookies—lots of them. She sent enough for the whole class, and she hid them under false bottoms in cardboard boxes so Staff Sergeant Carney wouldn't see them. Before she started doing this, he would make everyone eat them at mail call, which was always right after a hard cross-country run or obstacle-course workout. Eating cookies then made everyone feel sick. Mom's secret cookie scheme made us all laugh.

When we weren't eating smuggled cookies while studying at night, we were trying to survive the PT sessions, academics, and military drills. The drill instructor thrashed us all alike.

Each day a different person served as the class section leader. The section leader's job was to march the class between the events of the day. I was first up. I'd been in the marching band for several years in high school, so marching wasn't a problem for me. But the military used traditional call-and-response chants called jodies to keep a group marching in step. I didn't know even one jody. I did, however, remember lots of cheers from my days as a college cheerleader.

The drill instructor left me in charge. I knew where we needed to be and when we had to be there, so as the class formed up, I called out, "Forward, march." Once we were moving, I called out, "All right! All right! All right!"

The class yelled, "All right!"

"Okay! Okay! Okay!"

"Okay!"

"All right!"

"All right!"

"Okay!"

"Okay!"

And together we all shouted, "Navy all the way!"

When the drill instructors heard our cheer, they ran out of the battalion. I got through the routine a couple of times before they surrounded me and drowned out my voice with their own shouts. Staff Sergeant Carney fired me on the spot.

I was never allowed to serve as section leader again. For the rest of my time in AOCS, the drill instructors pulled me out of ranks and ordered me to do additional PT while they scolded me for marching a class of warriors with a college cheer.

In a strange way, the punishment was comforting. I felt like part of the gang anytime I was being screamed at. Soon enough the drill instructors would be yelling at someone else. The whole point of military boot camp is to break down individuals and build them back up as part of a team. I was happy to finally be on the team.

Physically and academically, I kept up with my classmates. I was never top of the class, but I was never altogether last either.

I was happy to finally be on the team.

With all of the demands of AOCS, I could not write much in my journals. Often I was so tired I just whispered a prayer and left my problems in God's hands before I fell asleep. I used prayer and journaling to keep things from rolling around in my mind and growing worse. This practice would become a lifelong habit.

Near the end of the program, we went through survival training, a weeklong battery of skill tests. First we were bussed to a rural area outside Pensacola, where we hiked in the sun for miles. We learned to live off the land and navigate with a compass and a chart.

Next up was the Helo Dunker, a huge steel barrel suspended over a swimming pool. Six at a time, we strapped into seats inside the dunker, then it dropped into the pool and flipped upside down. Our task was to get out of the barrel. This exercise taught us how to escape a helicopter during a crash in the water, known as *ditching*. We did it several times, once wearing blacked-out goggles to make it seem like nighttime. When someone accidentally kicked me in the face and knocked off my goggles, I had to do it all again.

The following day, we were introduced to the Dilbert Dunker, which would teach us how to escape a jet that had gone into the water. A cockpit was mounted on two rails that extended down into the pool. Wearing all of our flight gear, each of us took turns strapping into the cockpit. Then the cockpit slid down the rails, plunged into the pool, and flipped upside down. We had to unstrap from the seat and swim to the surface.

I had spent six summers as a lifeguard, taught swim

lessons, and even did some synchronized swimming, so I was comfortable being underwater for long periods of time. When it was my turn, I was ready to go. As I slid down the rails, I took a deep breath and braced for the impact. The cockpit hit the water, flipped upside down, and came to a stop. I quickly unclipped the two buckles at my waist. Then I reached for the two at my shoulders. One released, but the other was stuck. I couldn't get the release bar to move.

A piece of nylon webbing from my torso harness was jammed in the buckle. An instructor swam down to me and gave the buckle a couple of hard tugs. But the webbing stayed put. He didn't have an air tank, so he returned to the surface while I continued to hold my breath. A second diver appeared and yanked on the buckle until he ran out of air as well. Then he surfaced. I kept trying.

With most of the air inside my lungs gone, I thought, *Are you kidding me? I have survived AOCS and passed every test! I'm a week away from earning my commission and heading to flight school! I will not drown doing the easy stuff!*

I yanked one last time with all my might. The jammed webbing ripped out of the buckle. I lunged for the surface and came up on the back side of the machine. No one saw me. The entire class and both divers were on the other side of the dunker, yelling at the operator, "Pull it up! She's still down there! Pull it up!" They brought the dunker up, but I was gone. A hush came over the class, then they heard me gasping for breath on the other side of the pool.

Because the instructors hadn't seen me get out, they made me strap back in and do it again.

I made it through the rest of survival week—not necessarily unharmed, but unkilled.

During the final week of AOCS, my classmates and I became candidate officers. This meant we served as the leaders for the next class starting the program. I left the "secure your luggage to the bulkhead" shouting to my peers and focused my attention on teaching the new class how to march—this time with jodies rather than college cheers.

On graduation day, we wore our dress-white uniforms and became commissioned as officers in the United States Navy. We started at the lowest rank: ensign. After receiving our ensign bars, we lined up to receive a salute and then a handshake from our drill instructor, whom we now outranked. Each new ensign palmed a silver dollar and passed it off to the drill instructor during that handshake as a token of respect.

I had cleared the first hurdle. I'd been tested and tried, and I'd come out stronger. Plus I had gained skills and habits that would prove critical in my life ahead.

FLIGHT TRAINING SCHOOL

Starting flight training at Naval Air Station Corpus Christi, in Texas, was a little bit like starting high school. I was happy *and* nervous.

I was assigned to a *squadron* that had both Navy and Marine Corps pilots. The squadron was divided into smaller groups called flights. I was one of the few Navy students in my flight, and I was the only woman in the entire squadron. The guys I knew from AOCS had been assigned to another flight, so I rarely saw them.

The Marines in my flight had just finished Marine officer training together, so they knew each other. I felt like an outsider. It was 1985, a time when there were no female Marine *aviators*. I was unusual even within the Navy, the first branch of the US military to put women in jets. For the next two years, I would be the only female in any of my squadrons.

Training started with ground school. Before we ever got into an airplane, we learned the basics of *navigation* (how to find your way safely from one point to another in the sky), *aerodynamics* (the study of how a plane's wings, flaps, tail, and body create *lift* in the air), and *meteorology* (weather science—especially the effects of weather on flight). We also studied aircraft systems such as fuel, electrical, and *hydraulics*. (A plane's hydraulic system activates equipment for steering and landing.) We focused on systems for the Beechcraft T-34C Turbo Mentor, because that's the plane we'd be flying first. As part of training, we got familiar with the plane on the ground by doing thorough checks of the equipment.

Then the time came to just get in and fly—with an instructor, of course. The instructor would give us directions from the back seat and take over the controls if we did something wrong. My T-34 instructor was Captain Coston, a Marine. At first, he was one of the few people in my flight who actually spoke to me.

We went out to the plane for the first time on a blazing hot July day. Before every flight, a pilot has to complete all sorts of safety checklists. The first thing to do is the preflight inspection, which is a visual check to see if the airplane is in good condition for flying. I was so excited and nervous when I finished my preflight that I just jumped into the cockpit and strapped myself in.

From the seat behind me, Captain Coston laughed. "Tammie Jo," he said. "Look to your left. What do you see?" I'd left all my flight gear lying on the ramp. I climbed out, grabbed my gear, put on my helmet and survival vest, and strapped myself back in.

I was familiar with my next round of checklists because I'd gone over them again and again during my studies. I completed them easily, then started the engine. It came to life with a smooth whine.

The T-34 cockpit is set up like a Navy fighter jet, with the throttle on the left and the control stick in the middle, between the pilot's knees. Strapped to my right thigh was one of the most important parts of my flight gear: my kneeboard.

The kneeboard is a miniature desk with a clip to hold a notepad in place, a pencil on a lanyard, and room for notes. It even has a light for reading those notes in the dark. I'm a planner, so my kneeboard was full. I had written every word I should say to the air traffic controllers.

First, Clearance gave me my flight plan and my "squawk," the identification code that our aircraft would transmit. I talked to Ground next and received permission to taxi out onto the runway. Using the *rudder* pedals to steer, I made my way there. *This is happening,* I thought. *It's finally happening.*

My next communication was with Tower, who cleared me for takeoff. Tower also assigned me a direction, or heading, and an altitude where I could safely fly clear of other aircraft. I found the runway centerline and pushed up the throttle. Stepping on the right rudder to keep the plane straight, I directed the T-34 down the runway and watched my speed build. When we hit eighty-six knots—almost one hundred miles per hour—I eased the stick back to raise the nose. We were off!

From the ground, flying may look easy. But pilots are constantly thinking about a lot of details. During my first flight, my mind was so busy that I couldn't fully appreciate the moment until later that night.

Captain Coston graded me on everything I did, from how I completed my checklists to the decisions I made, and even my attitude. I would be graded this way for the next two years.

On that first flight, we headed to Waldron Field, a practice airport. The first order of business in learning how to fly is learning how to land. At Waldron I would practice *touch-and-goes*. After bringing the plane down low enough for the landing gear to touch the runway, I would add power and take off again without coming to a stop.

Captain Coston directed me where to go. As we approached Waldron Field, he took the controls

I eased the stick back to raise the nose. We were off!

so he could put my plane in the proper position for landing. To do this quickly, he rolled the plane upside down, then did the second half of a barrel roll. He emerged from the maneuver perfectly. It was the coolest thing I'd ever seen! He didn't explain the maneuver to me, but I took mental notes.

After demonstrating how to land the T-34, he handed over the controls and began talking me through the touch-and-go process. Initially my landings weren't pretty, but Captain Coston didn't seem concerned. "Focus on flying a precise pattern, and the landings will come," he told me.

The next day, Captain Coston and I retraced our route. Soon he said, "Okay, take me to Waldron Field." He left it up to me to find my way there.

No problem, I thought. I followed the landmarks, then performed the same maneuver he'd done to get into position. I rolled the plane upside down. Then I pulled the nose toward the ground as I turned toward the field. My half barrel roll wasn't as pretty as his, but I did come out right side up and basically headed in the right direction. I was pretty proud of myself.

But Captain Coston seemed caught off guard. He yelled through the entire maneuver. "What in the world?! What are you doing?!" He was even-tempered, so I felt bad that I'd upset him. I felt even worse about how that might affect my grade.

"Sir, I was entering the pattern like you showed me yesterday."

He remembered the *aerobatic* maneuver he had used the day before and started laughing. "I can see I'll have to be more careful about what I do in front of you," he said. Then he explained that I wasn't quite ready to perform those complex maneuvers.

Though Captain Coston was friendly, it was tougher to get to know the other pilots in my flight. Each time I walked into the *ready room*, which is basically the pilots' breakroom, conversations stopped. As soon as I walked out, I could hear the chatter start up again. I felt so alone.

One time I mentioned this to my mom. "Invite some guys to your place for dinner," she suggested. "That's always a good way to make friends."

"These men are in warrior mode!" I protested. "They won't want to eat dinner with a girl they don't even talk to."

"Well, if you want a friend, be a friend," she said. I loved my sweet mom, but she clearly didn't understand how hard it really was.

A couple of days later, I approached the ready room. I could hear Nelson Alberts, one of the biggest and funniest Marine students, talking about a birthday package he'd received from his parents. As I walked in behind him, everyone went silent. Nelson slowly turned around to face me. I said, "I'd be happy to make you a birthday dinner and cake. Why don't you bring four of your friends over? It'll be fun."

He just stared at me.

I turned and left. I couldn't believe what I'd just done! Why had I said that?

But the next day, Nelson approached me and handed me a slip of paper with four names on it. "Where do you live?" he asked.

So one evening, Nelson and four other Marines arrived at my door. They were lighthearted, happy to celebrate, and perfectly polite. They didn't stop talking the whole evening. No one explained why they hadn't talked to me before, but it didn't matter. The six of us became friends, and some of us studied together throughout Primary, Intermediate, and Advanced training.

A few weeks later, the time came for me to fly solo. I *briefed* my flight plan with Captain Coston, checked the weather, and gathered up my flight gear. Then I pre-flighted the T-34 and climbed into the cockpit—by myself. I worked through the same checklists, followed the same procedures, and taxied out to the same runway. I was doing all of the things I had done with my instructor, but it felt completely different.

I'm going flying, I thought, *and I'm the only one in this plane*. When you're alone at the controls, you grow a little taller.

When I was in the air, I felt like someone had left the gate open and I'd escaped. This was freedom! My oxygen mask didn't seal well due to the grin I couldn't wipe off my face. Surely I was a real pilot now.

But this was just the beginning. Over the next few

months, I learned how to fly instruments. This means flying without being able to see anything but the instruments in the cockpit, an important skill at night or in bad weather. I also learned to fly closely with other airplanes in *formation* and to perform aerobatics (those fun moves I tried out on Captain Coston before I knew what I was doing).

At the end of Primary, students go into one of three flight-training pipelines: jets, propeller aircraft, or helicopters. A student's grades and preferences as well as the Navy's needs determine which pipeline a student will enter.

I'd done well, made the Commodore's List of high-achieving trainees, and finished second in my class. When orders were handed out, I got my first choice: jets! My friend Nelson presented me with Marine dog tags and declared me an honorary Marine. My Marine name was Tammie Jo Billy Bob Bonnell. I wore the tags but refused to answer to such a name.

This was a good beginning.

Tammie Jo's PLANES

PRODUCED:	1953–1959
RETIRED / IN USE:	retired
PURPOSE:	training
TOP SPEED:	322 mph
RANGE BEFORE REFUELING:	815 miles
CLIMB RATE:	1,480 feet of altitude per minute
PEOPLE:	two
WEAPONS:	two fixed machine guns; optional flares, fire bombs, missiles, rocket pods
FUN FACTS:	• 30,000 landings guaranteed by builder • 40 gallons of fuel burned per hour

T-34 MENTOR

T-2 BUCKEYE

PRODUCED:	1959
RETIRED / IN USE:	retired
PURPOSE:	training
TOP SPEED:	518 mph
RANGE BEFORE REFUELING:	905 miles
CLIMB RATE:	6,200 feet of altitude per minute
PEOPLE:	two
WEAPONS:	practice bombs, machine gun pods, rocket pods
FUN FACTS:	• named for the Buckeye State of Ohio, where the plane was made • called "the Guppy" because it looks like a fat fish

PRODUCED:	1956
RETIRED / IN USE:	retired
PURPOSE:	combat
TOP SPEED:	645 mph
RANGE BEFORE REFUELING:	2,001 miles
CLIMB RATE:	10,300 feet of altitude per minute
PEOPLE:	one
WEAPONS:	two fixed cannons; optional cannons, missiles, rocket pods, nuclear weapons, bombs
FUN FACT:	nicknamed the "Credit Card" because the cockpit is extremely narrow

A-4 SKYHAWK

A-7 CORSAIR II

PRODUCED:	1967
RETIRED / IN USE:	retired
PURPOSE:	combat
TOP SPEED:	659 mph
RANGE BEFORE REFUELING:	564 miles
CLIMB RATE:	5,000 feet of altitude per minute
PEOPLE:	one
WEAPONS:	two fixed cannons; optional missiles, bombs, rocket pods
FUN FACT:	13,000 missions flown in the Vietnam War

PRODUCED:	1999
RETIRED / IN USE:	in use
PURPOSE:	combat
TOP SPEED:	1,187 mph
RANGE BEFORE REFUELING:	680 miles
CLIMB RATE:	44,890 feet of altitude per minute
PEOPLE:	one or two
WEAPONS:	standard cannon and two missiles; optional missiles, bombs, nuclear weapons, rocket pods
FUN FACT:	Pilots designed the cockpit, with advice from engineers, rather than the usual method—engineers designing with help from pilots.

F/A-18 HORNET

PRODUCED:	1967
RETIRED / IN USE:	retired
PURPOSE:	wartime observation; converted to forest-fire fighting
TOP SPEED:	200 mph
RANGE BEFORE REFUELING:	1,325 miles
CLIMB RATE:	1,180 feet of altitude per minute
PEOPLE:	two
WEAPONS:	none
FUN FACTS:	• During the Vietnam War, steel plates on the floor protected pilots from being shot from underneath. • Loudspeakers and flyer dispensers allowed the pilot to communicate with the enemy.

CESSNA O-2 SKYMASTER

PRODUCED:	1997
RETIRED / IN USE:	in use
PURPOSE:	commercial
TOP SPEED:	588 mph
RANGE BEFORE REFUELING:	5,063 miles
CLIMB RATE:	1,800 feet of altitude per minute
PEOPLE:	149 passengers
WEAPONS:	none
FUN FACT:	built to be able to land worldwide on runways of all sizes

BOEING 737-700

CESSNA 177 CARDINAL

PRODUCED:	1968–1978
RETIRED / IN USE:	in use
PURPOSE:	private
TOP SPEED:	144 mph
RANGE BEFORE REFUELING:	591 miles
CLIMB RATE:	670 feet of altitude per minute
PEOPLE:	four
WEAPONS:	none
FUN FACTS:	• Tammie Jo and Dean own a Cardinal. • The Cardinal is known for its visibility and is the choice of many aerial photographers.

INTERMEDIATE CHALLENGES

After Primary Flight Training, I went to Intermediate Jet Training. The Navy sent me to another base in Texas, Naval Air Station Beeville, for this stage.

The first jet I learned to fly there was the mighty T-2 Buckeye. The T-2 has never been considered the sleekest jet in the military's lineup. The plump-bodied Buckeye has straight wings with fuel tanks at the tips and dual engines along the belly of the aircraft. Because it looks like a fat little fish, the Buckeye is affectionately referred to as "the Guppy." But the T-2 has its virtues. It's solid and sturdy, built to take the hard pounding of landing on aircraft carriers (*trapping*) and taking off from them (*cat shots*).

Some of the T-2 training repeated what I learned in T-34s, but at much higher speeds. One of my favorite phases of flight training was *formation flying*, which is when groups of airplanes fly close together. It seemed to come naturally to me. In the T-34, we had learned to fly in a *section* of two aircraft. Now in jets, we flew in four-plane *divisions*. Formation flying is like being on a basketball team: it's fun to shoot hoops alone, but playing a game with others is much more exhilarating.

Things went well until I was assigned to fly with Captain Cornejo, a Venezuelan pilot doing an exchange tour in the United States. He had been a member of Venezuela's flight demonstration team, so he was an expert formation flyer. When he learned he had been assigned to fly with a female student, he felt insulted. On our first flight together, he came out to the plane while I was doing the preflight check. He was furious.

"Women don't fly!" he said to me. "There's a reason they don't fly!"

I gave him my attention but didn't respond.

"I tell them, I do not fly with females! Do you cry?"

"Not in the cockpit," I said as I climbed up and settled in.

He followed me, mounting the steps as if

> "I tell them, I do not fly with females! Do you cry?"
>
> "Not in the cockpit," I said.

he wanted to put his boots right through the plane. Then he dropped into the back seat, grumbling in Spanish. I didn't speak the language well enough to understand him, so his complaints were easier to ignore.

To his credit, Captain Cornejo had an open mind, and he had a change of heart. Apparently my formation skills impressed him. By the time we taxied in and shut down the aircraft, I had won him over. He even went to the scheduling office and requested to be my formation instructor for the duration of the program. I was incredibly fortunate to be his student. He had spent his career perfecting formation techniques, and he was a good instructor.

Air-to-air gunnery was the skill students tackled next. In that phase, we went out as a four-plane formation. Another T-2 towed a banner that represented an enemy aircraft. We flew in a pattern: each plane took quick turns rolling in from a high perch and maneuvering into position to shoot down the "enemy." Then that pilot moved out of the way for the next shooter. To have four aircraft flying this pattern together required carefully timed moves. This was *fun*.

Most phases of jet training involved multiple flights, but the out-of-control flight, or OCF, was a single outing. Before being allowed to fly solo, all students had to show that they could recover the aircraft from an out-of-control situation. This includes stalls (when the plane is traveling too slow to stay in flight) and spins (when the airplane falls downward like a leaf instead of flying straight). The only way to master this skill is to practice. We would fly to a high altitude and intentionally put the plane in a stall or spin over and over and over again. This is called *departing controlled flight.*

My OCF didn't frighten me, but it was unlike any other flying experience. Seated behind me, my instructor flew the T-2 to almost thirty thousand feet. Then he pulled the throttles back to idle and held the plane's nose on the horizon. In a few seconds, the plane's engine stopped and the nose dropped, just as he had told me it would. Then he gave the controls to me.

The feeling of falling was a little unsettling, but I relaxed pressure on the stick and pushed it forward. This allowed the aircraft to seek flight, gain speed, and stabilize. The T-2 responded, and I was in control again. That wasn't bad at all! My instructor took us back up, and we progressed from simple stalls to more complicated spins.

Up and down and around and around we went for about an hour. The OCF required about ten different departures from flight. When my instructor was satisfied that I knew what to do, we headed back to base and landed. My OCF was complete.

I could have lived on the base in Beeville, but I found a big house out in the country instead. Two young ladies from my church who were high school teachers became my roommates. I loved the open space and the independence. I studied when I wasn't flying, but I was starting to like my freedom. I decorated my home like I wanted and ate what I wanted.

One of the things I loved to eat was brownie mix. After training, I'd come home hungry and tired and not that interested in cooking dinner. I'd often pull a box of brownie mix out of the cabinet, prepare it as directed with eggs and oil, then eat the batter right out of the bowl.

I was flying twice a day most days, studying hard, playing softball on the squadron teams, and going to church. Soon the busy schedule caught up with me, though, and I started feeling run-down.

"I don't feel good," I told my mom one day when I called home. "I'm not sick. I just don't feel that great."

Ever practical, Mom asked me some questions about how much sleep and exercise I was getting. "What are you eating?" she eventually asked.

When I told her I was having brownie mix for dinner a few times a week, she suggested that I replace that with better nutrition before spending money on a doctor. Of course, Mom was right. As soon as I got rid of the junk food, I started feeling better.

I could almost hear Staff Sergeant Carney yelling at me: *Attention to detail, Bonnell!*

So I started paying more and more attention to the details, even the ones that didn't seem important at first, such as what I ate for dinner. There was nowhere I'd need to pay attention to detail more than when I learned to land my T-2 on an aircraft carrier.

THE AIRCRAFT
CARRIER

Knowing how to land safely on an aircraft carrier is the skill that sets Navy pilots apart. It's one of the most challenging tasks naval aviators perform. A thousand details have to come together. And missing even one of them can be a matter of life or death. This phase of training forged a new set of nerves in me.

The carrier is the Navy's largest ship, and it's like an airport in the middle of the ocean. From on board, an aircraft carrier seems huge. And it is—it's almost as long as three football fields. But to a pilot high in the sky, it looks about as big as a postage stamp—a stamp bobbing on the waves. With each swell of the ocean, the deck of the carrier rises and falls, rolling from side to side and front to back. It's an ever-moving target.

The initial practice took place on a nice, stable runway with a carrier landing zone painted on it. Beside the runway was what we called the *meatball*, a light system that shows pilots if they're on the proper *glide slope*, or path to landing. Landing Signal Officers (LSOs) stood beside the runway and talked to us on the radio as we approached, just as they would on the aircraft carrier. We practiced this way twice a day for a few weeks: we would take off from the base, turn directly into the landing pattern, and do touch-and-goes until we needed more gas. We made hundreds of passes, always checking our position and speed and making corrections. We never settled for less than perfection, though that also seemed to be a moving target.

There was no carrier landing simulator for the T-2. So the first time I got a picture of what an aircraft carrier looked like from behind was when it was time to actually land on it—and a pilot's first carrier landing is a solo landing! The joke is that they can't pay anyone enough to sit in your back seat the first time you go to the boat. The truth is that a student needs to be 100 percent focused, not worried about what an instructor in the back seat is thinking. For this important

We never settled for less than perfection.

carrier qualification, the instructor is the LSO standing to the side of the flight deck.

My first good look at the carrier I would land on, the USS *Lexington*, was from several thousand feet in the sky. The tower on the flight deck, called the island, is the carrier's command center. The *Lexington*'s flight deck was divided into two sections. The front half, from the island to the *bow*, had two *catapults* for launching aircraft. The back half, extending to the *stern*, consisted of a landing area. This design allowed landings and launches to happen at the same time.

From above, I could see the tiny landing deck with four thick cables, called wires, strung across it. I would try to grab one of these cables with my plane's tailhook. This kind of landing is called a trap. If I failed to follow proper procedures, I could keep going right off the other end of the carrier.

I waited my turn to land along with three other students. Off to the *starboard* (right) side of the ship, a helicopter flew in a loose holding pattern. If a pilot ejected, its crew would fish the aviator out of the water.

Even with all that landing practice back at the field, my heart beat like a racehorse's hooves. When it was my turn to go in, I slowed down hard and put my landing gear and flaps down. Then I put the tailhook down.

I came in at eight hundred feet above the water. I held that altitude through a turn, then descended to six hundred feet until it was time to start the final descending turn. If I did this right, I'd roll out behind the boat right on glide slope.

About halfway through my approach turn, I saw the meatball out the left side of my window. It was slightly high and settling into the center, which meant I was right on glide slope. The LSO said over the radio, "One twenty-six, call the ball."

"One twenty-six, Buckeye ball, six-point-two," I said, indicating my plane's number, aircraft type, and fuel state in thousands of pounds. Knowing the fuel state of every aircraft around the carrier is critical, particularly in a training environment. They never want an aircraft to run low on gas.

The LSO guided me in, calling adjustments I needed to make. I kept checking my position, kept making tiny corrections, all the way to touchdown.

Wham!

I landed with a jolt. The next thing I knew, I was hanging in the straps of my torso harness as I came to a sudden stop.

A carrier pilot always has to be ready for things that could go wrong. On touchdown, I had shoved the throttles full forward just in case my tailhook hadn't caught a wire. That would have given me the power to fly off the carrier, go around, and try again.

On my first attempt, however, I caught a wire. I had my first trap!

There was no time to savor the moment. Each aircraft

was spaced about one minute behind the aircraft ahead. This allowed just enough time for a plane to disengage from the cable and taxi out of the landing area while the crew reset the cable for the next landing. It was poetry in motion in one of the most dangerous work environments in the world.

A yellow shirt (plane captain) gave me the signal to throttle back to idle and keep my feet off the brakes. I felt a tug backward as the crew retracted the arresting cable. The yellow shirt gave me the signal to raise my hook and move out of the way. One of my classmates was about to land. I cleared the area and was passed off to another yellow shirt, who gave me taxi directions toward the bow of the ship. My first carrier landing was a success, but the celebration would have to wait.

Next up was my first catapult launch off the carrier, the cat shot. With multiple yellow shirt hand signals directing me, I lined up the T-2 with one of the *Lexington*'s two catapults. When directed, I lowered the launch bar on the nose gear of my jet, and the catapult crew secured the plane into the catapult's shuttle. Behind the jet, they raised the blast deflector, a protective wall, as I confirmed my aircraft's weight. On their signal I put my throttles to full power. I could feel the pull as the catapult's tension was applied to my jet.

Next, I gave the shooter (the officer in charge of operating the catapults) a sharp salute, signaling that I was ready to go. He looked down the catapult track one more time to make sure it was clear. Then he returned my salute and pushed a button that launched me like a rocket. I accelerated from zero to about 150 miles an hour in two and a half seconds. It felt like someone had kicked me in the backside! Legend has it that the *Lexington*'s catapults can sling a Volkswagen Beetle more than a mile. I don't know if that's true, but I'm inclined to believe it.

The deck of an aircraft carrier sits about sixty feet above the water, and the cat shot sends a jet straight off the bow of the ship. Sixty feet is about the height of a six-story building, which might seem pretty high, but it's quite low for a plane taking off. We'd been warned not to climb too high after the launch. At that low altitude, if a pilot raised the nose too fast and stalled, there would be no chance of recovering the jet. Besides, the instructors teased, "It makes you look like you're afraid of the water."

I didn't want to look like a sissy, so after the cat shot, I kept flying straight ahead about sixty feet off the surface . . . for a while. The feeling of being launched was so intense, I guess I was lost in the moment, intensely scanning my instruments. My instructor took note of my low flight. Afterward, he left a scribbled joke in my logbook: "Check intakes for mackerel."

Tammie Jo and Dwight
on Honey, 1964

Tammie Jo's
prekindergarten
picture, 1965

Mom, Sandra, Dwight, Dad,
and Tammie Jo, Florida
Mesa, Colorado, 1967

Dad at High Nogal Ranch, Tularosa, New Mexico, 1974

Tammie Jo's first 4-H calf, George, a Brangus steer, 1974

Tammie Jo, Sandra, and D'Shane welcoming a new baby calf

Tammie Jo after her eighth grade honors banquet, Tularosa, New Mexico

Rascal, Tammie Jo's German shepherd, who loved to run with her horse, Peanuts

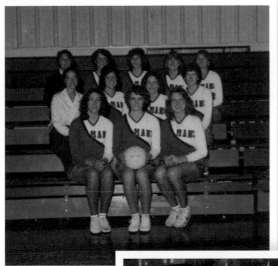

MidAmerica
Nazarene College
volleyball team,
1981 (Tammie Jo,
front row left)

MidAmerica Nazarene
College cheer team,
1982 (Tammie Jo,
third from right,
was team captain
her senior year.)

Tammie Jo, javelin
throw at a senior-year
track meet, 1983

Tammie Jo being sworn in to the Navy at Western New Mexico University, 1985

Tammie Jo's Aviation Officer Candidate School boot camp graduation, no smiling allowed, 1985

Tammie Jo in full flight gear, 1986

Tammie Jo in the front cockpit of an A-4 Skyhawk, flying an approach in formation, 1987

Navy flight training is complete, 1987

Tammie Jo with Bill Calvert, Air Combat Maneuvers (ACM) partner, in front of the A-4 Skyhawk

ACM instructor congratulating Tammie Jo

Flight line traditional ceremony commemorating Tammie Jo's last training flight

Tammie Jo on the wing of an A-4 Skyhawk, 1987

Dean and Tammie Jo in a pre-wedding photo with an A-4 in the background, 1988

Tammie Jo and Dean walking through the traditional military sword arch on their wedding day, November 26, 1988

A-7 aircraft from Tammie Jo's VAQ-34 Flashback squadron, transiting to mission, 1989

A-3 Whale with two A-7 Corsairs in formation, 1989

Dean and Tammie Jo
in front of a freshly
painted F/A-18 Hornet,
VFA-27, 1991

Tammie Jo, Sue Hart,
and Linda Heid Maloney
on detachment,
Puerto Rico, 1992

Brenda Scheufele, Tammie Jo, and Pam Lyons Carel,
Navy Times, May 10, 1993

Family flight, with Dean in the pilot's seat

The family's first backpacking camping trip, Enchanted Rock, Fredericksburg, Texas, 2000

Sydney, Dean, and Marshall on a hunting trip (while avoiding alligators), south of San Antonio, 2006

Sydney, Tammie Jo, and Marshall at a family ski vacation, Brighton, Utah, 2007

Sydney, Tammie Jo, and Marshall, 2007

Superhero Theme Night, T Bar M, New Braunfels, Texas, August 2010

Marshall and Sydney, 2015 (Marshall is smiling only because he's holding a popsicle on Sydney's back; she never flinched.)

Dean, Tammie Jo, and Marshall, Aztec, New Mexico, 2016

Tammie Jo and Marshall at javelin practice, prep for Texas Relays, March 2017

The world as seen through Sandra's eyes

The VAQ Girls: Tammie Jo, Pam Lyons Carel, Rosemary Mariner, Sue Hart, Brenda Scheufele, and Linda Heid Maloney, Boerne, Texas, May 25, 2005

Kandy Johnson Hintor, Jasmine Pagan, Sydney, and Tammie Jo in her Cessna 177 RG Cardinal, summer 2017

Captain Rosemary Mariner, Tammie Jo, and Captain Tommy Mariner; Rosemary's induction into the Women in Aviation Hall of Fame, summer 2017

Dean and Lexi Lou, the Shults's adopted axis deer, December 2017

Tammie Jo and her mom, December 2017

Morning tea with the gang: Little Bit (white-tail deer rescued by Sydney), Critter the cat, and Sadie Mae the Brittany spaniel, June 2018

View of the damaged engine, cowling, and wing from the galley door of Flight 1380

View of the exposed engine from Flight 1380; pieces of the cowling were found below the flight path

Captain Tammie Jo Shults and First Officer Chris
Hall, May 16, 2018 (her first flight after Flight 1380)

Seanique Mallory, Kathryn Sandoval, Darren Ellisor,
Tammie Jo, and Rachel Fernheimer, Flight 1380 crew, just
prior to *CBS Morning Show* interview, May 23, 2018

WHAT ARE CALL SIGNS?

A call sign is a nickname given by a pilot's peers and used during flights. It can be based on a pilot's last name, such as Tammie Jo's call sign, Bonnie. Before she married, Tammie Jo's last name was Bonnell. Her first jets instructor had the call sign Clyde, so the other pilots dubbed Tammie Jo "Bonnie." When the schedule listed them together as "Bonnie and Clyde," they looked like the famous bank robbers. Tammie Jo's friend Pam Lyons was called Dandy, to make the word *dandelions*. A call sign can also come from a physical trait. One guy with a large head was called Noggin. But most call signs come from an embarrassing moment. One pilot was called Boom-Boom after blowing out his plane's tires during a landing. Weeds got his call sign from running his plane off the runway and into a nearby field.

ENEMY TERRITORY

Not long after my successful carrier landing, I met my first real opponent: the operations officer—we called him the Ops O—at the squadron where I was assigned to my Advanced Flight Training. He had a reputation for being unfair to women. The Ops O was the squadron's third in command, and his authority meant that disobeying his orders would bring serious consequences, such as being disciplined or even booted out of the flight program.

My jet for this advanced phase was the Douglas A-4 Skyhawk, a plane you couldn't fly without feeling really cool. The A-4 was a true combat jet that saw service in the Vietnam War. It was a serious attack aircraft.

As in Primary and Intermediate training, we went to

ground school first, then had sessions in instrument simulators, then started doing local flights. After that, we started flying cross-country, making longer flights over weekends. Cross-country flights were like road trips. They were an opportunity to practice flight planning, flying by instruments, and shooting approaches to unfamiliar airports.

An added bonus was the chance to get away for a weekend—and in an A-4, you could get a long way in a hurry. Typically, an instructor and a student planned the trip together. Maybe they'd go out to San Diego, California, home of the Navy Fighter Weapons School (*TOPGUN*) and the F-14 Tomcat squadrons. Or maybe they'd go to the student's hometown to show Mom and Dad the new jet. While a cross-country trip was serious training, it could also be some serious fun.

As the time for my cross-country approached, however, I was surprised to get a summons to the Ops O's office. I was more than a little nervous. I'd never met him, and he wasn't my usual instructor. When I arrived, he told me he would be my instructor for the cross-country. He handed me a sheet of paper with the information I needed to plan the trip, then dismissed me.

The whole arrangement was strange. My friends had heard of his reputation and were alarmed. They warned me that nothing good would come from doing my cross-country with him. I didn't know what to do and actually prayed that he might get sick and have to bow out.

Instead, I was the one who got sick. On the Friday we

were scheduled to leave, I woke up with a terrible sinus infection and a full-blown fever. My cross-country trip had to be rescheduled, and that time I went with my usual instructor. But it seemed the Ops O was upset with me.

One day an *enlisted* para rigger, one of the guys who packed parachutes and maintained important flight gear, pulled me aside. He whispered, "If you need to get a custom torso harness made, there's a place out in China Lake where you can get it done."

The torso harness is a seatbelt-like piece of flight equipment that pilots wear. It attaches them to their ejection seats. Mine, though not a perfect fit, seemed just fine. I didn't know why the para rigger was telling me this. China Lake was all the way out in California.

A few days later the ready room was full of instructors and students when the Ops O walked in. He stood about ten feet away from me and loudly announced, "Bonnell, you're going to have to check out of the jet pipeline and go fly props."

The place fell silent, and I felt like the world was staring at me. He was kicking me out of the jets program!

"Sir?" I asked, hoping for an explanation.

"Your torso harness doesn't fit," he explained. "We can't have you flying around in something that might injure you if you eject." He spoke as if it was a done deal. He was sending me to the pipeline for propeller aircraft, and that was all there was to it.

I was stunned. Then I remembered the hushed advice

of the para rigger. I said, "Sir, I was told the guys who need a custom-fit harness just go out to China Lake and have one made in a day."

The Ops O didn't respond. He simply turned and walked out. I glanced around and caught the sympathetic eyes of a few of my friends, who were shaking their heads in disbelief. I was just grateful that someone—thank you, para riggers!—had seen what was coming and warned me.

He was kicking me out of the jets program!

I went to California and had the harness made, and that was the last I heard of it. While it was clearly not his intent, the Ops O had actually done me a favor. The new custom harness fit much better than my old one.

But I had a running battle with head colds that I couldn't kick. During one night flight, I went out with a stuffy nose. Suddenly, I felt as if someone had shoved an ice pick through my forehead. The pain was excruciating for a moment, then it eased up. I pressed on, but after more painful flights, I knew I was getting worse. I would have to see the *flight surgeon*.

My diagnosis was not good. Flying congested, I'd blown an upper sinus; then that sinus became infected. The flight surgeon grounded me until it healed.

Normally a pilot in my condition was allowed bed rest, which is what the doctor initially recommended. But the Ops O ordered me to desk duty. Instead of getting solid sleep, I had to man the squadron duty desk for a twelve-hour shift every other night, from 8:00 p.m. to 8:00 a.m.

While on duty, I was supposed to be alert and ready because I was the point of contact for an emergency. That first night I felt anything but alert and ready. I was sick to my stomach, and my head pounded. All I wanted to do was curl up and sleep. A night stretched into a week. Then a week turned into a month. Then one month became two. I simply could not get better.

My journals during that stretch of life reflect that I was down. Not just *med down*, but depressed. I felt like I was being left behind as I watched my class, and even classes behind mine, move on through the program.

I had to remind myself I was more than what I did. I had worth in God's eyes regardless of whether I was med up or med down. It didn't matter whether the Ops O liked me or not or even whether I was a naval aviator or not. At one point I wrote: *God, I fear I'm forgetting much and forgetting my battle to be who I am without apology for being a woman. You made me, and I know there is a reason You made me a girl.* Even then I knew that what I'd been given was sacred—from the color of my eyes to my gender to my faith to my love of flying. Everything that made me *me* was a gift, and I needed to treat it that way.

Two months turned into three.

Finally, mercifully, my blown sinus healed. I was able to pick up where I'd left off, although I was pretty rusty and a few months behind schedule. All of my friends in the program had finished and pinned on their wings of gold. They were full-fledged naval aviators, off learning how to fly their assigned fleet aircraft. I was still in Beeville surrounded by students I didn't know. No doubt I was down, but I was nowhere near out.

WHO ARE NAVY SQUADRON LEADERS?

Navy squadrons are local units. They typically have three layers of command.

Title	Nickname	Officer Rank
1. Commanding Officer	CO or Skipper	Commander
2. Executive Officer	XO	Commander
3. Department Heads • Operations Offlcer (missions) • Maintenance Officer (aircraft and its systems) • Intelligence Officer (clearance) • Administration Officer (paperwork)	Ops O	Lieutenant Commander

Other military branches are similarly organized, but the officers have different titles and ranks.

US NAVY
OFFICER RANK STRUCTURE

ENSIGN

LIEUTENANT JUNIOR GRADE

LIEUTENANT

LIEUTENANT COMMANDER

COMMANDER

CAPTAIN

REAR ADMIRAL LOWER HALF

REAR ADMIRAL UPPER HALF

VICE ADMIRAL

ADMIRAL

FLEET ADMIRAL

DOGFIGHTS

As a child, I'd watched the T-38s dogfight in the skies over my family's ranch. Now it was my turn.

Aerial Combat Maneuvering (ACM), or dogfighting, is the most dynamic flying I have ever done. In ACM, the object is to take out, or shoot down, an enemy aircraft coming in at top speed.

In training, basic ACM starts with two aircraft flying parallel to each other but a mile apart. At the "Fight's on!" call, they turn in and fly toward each other until they pass. At that point, it becomes a high-speed, three-dimensional, twisting, turning match, with each pilot jockeying for position behind the other. If a pilot is able to saddle up behind his opponent and get the aircraft's gunsight on the other jet, the call over the radio is "Guns!" It's a call you always want to make and never want to hear. These engagements don't usually last long and often end in a draw when either jet hits the hard deck, an altitude of ten thousand feet.

Because the sinus infections had delayed me, there was only one other student in the ACM phase when I got there. A friend of mine, Bill Calvert, became my opponent in the air. Bill and I studied together on the ground so that we would both be better fighters. He and his wife, Lori, often invited me over to their home for dinner. Bill and I would talk through the next flight, and when we thought we were ready, Lori would quiz us.

Bill's gunsight spent a fair amount of time on my jet, but in one particular face-off that stands out in my memory, I did get guns on him.

We had done our head-on pass and pulled up. We flew up into the sun, then came down again, a tactical move that causes an opponent to lose sight of you. About halfway through the engagement, Bill and I were tangled up in a flat scissors. That means we had our jets' noses parked high in the air, flying as slowly as possible without stalling, as we weaved back and forth trying to get behind each other.

I thought I had enough space to turn in behind him, but I misjudged. I had to think fast because I was shooting out in front. I dipped the plane's nose a little more, gained airspeed, then did a barrel roll over the top of him.

This move caused me to lose airspeed—just the amount I needed to come up right behind him. My instructor let out a whoop and said, "Guns!" Bill, always gracious, had a chuckle at my save.

During the last few ACM flights, the weather turned foggy. Bad weather meant I was required to have a safety observer riding in the back seat. I didn't mind—until I learned it was the Ops O. Though he was strictly there as a safety precaution and was only supposed to observe, he did his best to distract and discourage me. His presence tested my ability to separate his insults and criticisms from what I needed to do. I came to think of him as a coral snake. He had no real fangs. He would just chew on a person until he could break the skin to introduce his venom.

Because he outranked my instructor, the Ops O insisted on having a say in my grades. One day he gave me a below-average mark for the way I had the sleeves of my flight suit rolled, even though there was no standard for this. The next day he screamed a few times for no other reason than to be distracting. He gave me another below-average mark because my voice was "too high."

During Advanced Jet Training, it seemed I was constantly facing challenges like this—not the good challenges of conquering the flight program, but daily struggles to defend my right to be in it. I dealt with these struggles by praying about them and writing in my journal. This habit saved me from having to carry offenses around with me or burdening my friends at the squadron with my complaints.

It also became clear to me that I was being opposed by individuals, *not* an organization. Some dishonest people misused their authority and wielded their personal beliefs as weapons. But they didn't represent everyone. The Navy had opened the door for me to be in the program, even if certain individuals within the Navy didn't want me there.

When you're an underdog, it's easy to see yourself as a victim. But sometimes trials are just trials. Once, an instructor failed me during a formation exercise for a "dangerous" maneuver, even though the safety observer in my back seat thought it was one of the best moves he'd ever seen. I'd never been failed for anything in flight training, and at first I was crushed! But as I thought about it, I realized the instructor had to use his own judgment. His opinion was different from mine, and even different from those of other instructors. I didn't think my move was dangerous, but I was there to learn. I followed his instructions, repeated the exercise, and pressed on.

Doing the right thing wasn't always easy. One day I was scheduled for two ACM flights. After the first one ended, I wrote down my flight time in the maintenance logbook. Then I went upstairs to debrief and get a cup of tea. Before I even sat down, I got a call from maintenance asking me to verify my flight time. I grabbed my kneeboard card

When you're an underdog, it's easy to see yourself as a victim.

and headed back downstairs. The maintenance officer wasn't there, but one of his petty officers suggested that the time I'd written down was off. I double-checked my notes and confirmed that what I had entered was accurate. He hinted again that it probably wasn't.

I soon realized this had nothing to do with the accuracy of my entry. It had everything to do with the petty officer wanting me to put a different, lower time in the logbook. I assured him again that I had written the correct times. He finally said if I didn't change the record, they'd have to pull the jet out of service to do a scheduled inspection. That meant they might not have enough jets for our next ACM *sortie*. It would be my fault if they had to cancel our next flight.

I refused to be bullied. "My times are correct," I told him. "If the plane is due to be inspected, then it's due."

Interestingly, there were enough jets available to fly our second sortie that day. When I walked into maintenance later to fill out the logbook after my second flight, I was told the maintenance master chief, an important authority figure, wanted to see me. I mentally prepared to be chewed out for disagreeing with his petty officer. To my surprise, in front of the entire crew, including the gentleman who had wanted me to change my logbook entry, the chief told me they'd inspected the plane and found a critical part missing.

"I'm amazed that engine stayed together at all," he said. "It sure wouldn't have stayed together through another ACM flight." He turned to me. "You did the right thing."

I finished Advanced Flight Training near the top of my class again. My last flight ended with a splash—it was the squadron's tradition to dump a bucket of ice water over the heads of students who finish the program.

It was also a tradition for any available squadron leaders to come out on the ramp for the last-flight celebration. I don't know if the Ops O was there or not. It didn't matter anymore. I couldn't help but feel I had won that battle.

OUT OF CONTROL

Having graduated with high grades, I was invited by my Intermediate Jet Training commander to stay in Beeville and return to his squadron as an instructor pilot (IP). I considered this offer an honor and accepted.

After earning my wings, I rewarded myself with a German shepherd puppy and named him Huckleberry. Huck was a furry bundle of joy in my life. I started rushing home after work just to see him. My four-legged friend greeted me at the back screen door every day with a happy face and a wagging tail. He became my friend and study partner. He curled up beside me while I hit the books as a new IP.

My first year passed without a hitch. I enjoyed

teaching new students how to fly the T-2 Buckeye, and life was good. Then the squadron had a change of command.

The new skipper was no fan of women in his Navy. When the time came for me to get my advanced qualifications so I could start teaching air-to-air gunnery, he refused to let me do it—even though I had already completed the class and passed the required test.

When I told the Ops O what was happening, he said, "Girls don't do guns in the skipper's Navy."

"Sir, you know that isn't fair," I said.

"Give it up, Bonnell. Write me up for discrimination if you want to."

I could write him up, of course. But my complaint would go right up the same chain of command that had made the decision. This upset me, and I had to remind myself that life isn't always fair. In the grand scheme of life, it was a minor setback.

After a week or so, I went directly to the skipper to plead my case, hoping to convince him to change his mind. Instead, he slapped me with a penalty. He assigned me to teach the out-of-control flight (OCF).

As I've mentioned, no one likes the OCF, but all students have to pass it before they can fly solo. One reason this flight is dreaded is that students often throw up all over the cockpit. Also, the physical demands of the flight are so tough that IPs are only allowed to do one OCF per day.

Teaching this program became my lot for the next year, however, so I decided to do my best. It was my responsibility as the IP to make sure we got through the flight safely, so I studied the Navy OCF manual and memorized every recovery listed. Our lives depended on it.

Everyone else disliked this job. It was physically draining, but eventually I found it rewarding. I liked helping students develop a skill they dreaded learning. Many were so anxious about the flight that they were already greenish and swallowing hard during the brief! Since I helped clean up the cockpit whenever my students threw up, I was motivated to find a solution.

Fortunately I found one. Students tended not to eat anything before the flight because they believed this would keep them from vomiting. But we had to fly with our oxygen masks on from takeoff to touchdown, and breathing 100 percent oxygen under pressure on an empty stomach is sure to make a pilot feel queasy. I started encouraging my students to eat *something*, ideally a peanut butter sandwich, before the brief. Then I'd promise them that after we finished the requirements of the flight, we would burn the rest of our gas doing something fun, like acrobatics or sightseeing. It worked! That was pretty much the end of messy cockpits on my flights. Being able to conquer OCF without "blowing chow" made my students stand a little taller.

> I liked helping students develop a skill they dreaded learning.

Throughout that challenging year, I stayed focused on who I was and what I'd come to do. I think it's no coincidence that I met my future husband, Dean, during this time. He never saw me as a woman who was unhappy with her life—because I chose not to be.

I'd always wanted to marry and have a family, but I wasn't going to sit around and wait for it to happen. There was too much to learn and do! I volunteered as a Sunday school teacher, did woodworking projects, played my flute, and sang in the choir. And I sat outdoors with Huck whenever I had some free time, reading books and drinking sweet tea.

In January 1988, Dean was a pilot just starting Intermediate Jet Training. We met at church on a Sunday morning, but he didn't know until he reported to his squadron on Monday that I was an IP there. We saw each other regularly on base and at church, but we didn't really get to know each other until he needed to do a cross-country flight and his usual instructor couldn't go. Dean wanted to go to New Mexico, where his dad had a cabin. When he heard I'd grown up there, he asked if I'd be willing to stand in for his IP. I agreed.

On the trip, it became clear we had a lot in common. Both of us lived on tight budgets, so we ate toasted cheese sandwiches and fruit at the cabin instead of eating out. As we talked, we discovered we were going through the same read-the-Bible-in-a-year program. We talked about home, faith, college, and our journeys into aviation. We started calling each other by our first names.

We went skiing for the next two days. Because we didn't have ski gear, we wore our one-piece flight suits with long underwear underneath. Dean cracked jokes, we raced down the slopes, and we hung out with some other pilots from the squadron. We laughed a lot.

I had already graded a few of Dean's flights, and he had done well. He paid careful attention to the details, and it was a pleasure to instruct him. On the morning of our second day of skiing, Dean showed up with a hand-made evaluation sheet grading my skiing.

"It's only fair," he told me.

After that weekend, we started finding excuses to do things together. Our talks grew longer. We played racquetball and went to the same Bible study. For our first official date, Dean took me to a concert given by pianist George Winston. We watched classic black-and-white movies on the weekends and soon met each other's families. In July, during a visit to his aunt and uncle's place in Texas, Dean took me out for a moonlight boat ride on a river and asked me to marry him. He had bought an engagement ring all the way back in March and kept it hidden for four months! I was amazed and deeply in love.

We decided to have the wedding on Thanksgiving weekend. We were reaching the time when the Navy would give both of us new orders, and military detailers try to assign married couples as close to each other as possible.

Our church and friends helped with preparations. My mom made the butter mints, pralines, and satin flowers that held birdseed for guests to toss with their farewells. Dean's mom bought the only floral arrangement other than my bouquet. My parents paid for my dress, which I designed and had sewn by a talented seamstress in Brownsville.

Just weeks before the wedding, I took a student up for his out-of-control flight. It was clear he was prepared, and it was a beautiful day. Once we were at altitude, I started with a simple maneuver designed to get him used to the strange feeling of a stall entry. I pulled the power to idle and held altitude as the airspeed bled off. Then the rudder pedals shuddered, and the stall warning horn sounded. At this point, the nose of the plane should have dropped easily for a simple recovery. Instead, the plane whipped down and around, and the nose pointed straight at the ground.

We were at about twenty-eight thousand feet when the plane entered a spiral. We'd practiced spins, where the belly of the plane stays parallel to the ground. We had *not* practiced spirals, where the plane heads straight down, twisting like a drill bit. A T-2

Instead, the plane whipped down and around, and the nose pointed straight at the ground.

isn't supposed to be able to spiral, so there was no procedure in the Navy OCF manual for getting out of one!

I took control of the aircraft immediately, and my student called out the altitude in thousands of feet: "Twenty-five."

I tried every combination of recovery inputs, but nothing worked.

"Twenty. Nineteen. Eighteen. Seventeen . . ."

The plane ignored my efforts as it gained speed. The instruments became a blur, and the plane vibrated and rattled. The noise grew fierce.

"Fourteen. Thirteen. Twelve! *Eleven!*" We hurtled toward the ground at about four hundred miles per hour.

I tried everything I could think of. We passed ten thousand feet.

If we weren't in control by the time we hit five thousand, we would have to eject. The ejection procedures flashed through my mind. The back seat (mine) would fire a split second ahead of the front seat so we wouldn't hit each other in the air.

He belted out the altitude a little more shrilly: *"Eight! Seven! Six!"*

My mind was racing as fast as the spiraling plane, but my thoughts came evenly and clearly. *Really, God? I'm getting married soon, and ejections are messy! I'll be a cut and bruised bride that would frighten Frankenstein! I'll be a monster in a big white dress for all my wedding photos!*

I was so annoyed that I stomped hard on the rudders. Left! Right! Left! I threw the stick forward and reached for the ejection handle.

The plane wobbled out of the spiral.

"Don't. Touch. Anything." I said in my most calm and authoritative voice. My student had the same ejection handles that I did, and I thought he might reach for them.

Our T-2 leveled off well below five thousand feet, but we were flying in control again. All was smooth for a moment. Neither of us said a word. Then I thought, *If we don't complete this OCF, he's going to have a hard time getting back in the air to do it again.* So I briefed him as we climbed back up. I told him he may have added some flight control inputs that he wasn't aware of that prompted us to spiral.

"Let's try it again," I instructed.

He didn't say anything—I couldn't blame him—but he didn't object either.

We flew back up and started over. This time the plane did a lovely, wonderful, just-what-you'd-expect stall. He recovered in textbook style, and we continued with the OCF. We went through the rest of the departures without any surprises.

When we landed, he bent down and kissed the ground. Right then and there, in front of God and everyone. I also kissed the ground, but I waited until I was out of sight so I wouldn't scare my next student!

It took some doing to figure out why the T-2 had

spiraled. We finally found a pilot at the Navy's test-pilot school, NAS Patuxent River, who had an idea that turned out to be correct. The pilot said the T-2 could spiral if the jet wasn't properly balanced. With some investigation, and help from maintenance, we learned that one of the fuel valves was sticking. This caused the fuel in the tank on that wingtip to burn off at a slower rate. When we did our first stall, there were about five hundred more pounds of fuel at the end of that wing.

Patuxent River sent me the recovery procedures for a spiral, and I committed them to memory. And a few weeks later, I walked down the aisle to be married to Dean, happy not to be a monster bride.

AGGRESSOR SQUADRON

After I finished my tour as an instructor and Dean earned his aviator wings, the Navy sent us to California, but not to the same cities. Dean's orders were to a squadron in Lemoore, in the center of the state. I was assigned to Point Mugu, a coastal base 250 miles south of Lemoore and north of Los Angeles.

My squadron, officially known as VAQ-34, was an aggressor squadron. We existed to help the rest of the fleet practice their skills. We simulated enemy aircraft and missiles and "attacked" our own ships as well as other aircraft. Our fake attacks helped train combat pilots and the ships' weapons systems operators. We were electronic aggressors, which meant we carried jamming pods to disrupt our opponent's communication systems and imitated enemy *radar* signals. In other words, we played the bad guys. VAQ-34 was one of two naval squadrons at the time where females could fly *tactical aircraft*, which meant they had weapons on board. But we could not fly them in combat squadrons.

For the next couple years, Dean and I were seldom together for more than a few days at a time. A week at the most. I was gone on short-term assignments to Hawaii, Puerto Rico, and Miramar for several weeks at a time. He was out at sea for six months. We had no cell phones or e-mail—nothing except landline phones and letters to communicate. I was always flying one place while he flew somewhere else. In between flights, we talked on the phone—if we could find one.

In spite of the distance from Dean, I was happy about my assignment to VAQ-34. My squadron's executive officer (XO) was Commander Rosemary Mariner. She had been in the first class of women in the Navy, earning wings of gold in 1974. Ever since then, she had been a champion of *people*, not just women. Her brilliance and commitment to getting the job done were the key qualities of her leadership. One of the things I admired most about her was that she calmly responded to every person and situation with thoughtfulness.

The squadron also had other ladies of different ranks and occupations. I had never been attached to a squadron with other females, so it was nice not to be the odd woman out for once. As the squadron's ranking number two officer, Commander Mariner, along with the commanding officer, made Point Mugu a great place to work.

Training for aggressor missions involved several steps. The first was Electronic Warfare School, which was in a windowless building behind a fence topped with razor wire. There my brain was packed with data about the electronic warfare technology and capabilities of Russian, French, and Chinese weapons systems. We studied these nations because they were the weapons suppliers to most of the bad guys around the world at the time.

When that training ended, I went to SERE (Survival, Evasion, Resistance, and Escape) School. The first few days focused on how to survive and escape the enemy—that is, how *not* to become a prisoner of war (POW). The last few days were about how to survive as a POW. We learned methods for resisting the enemy and also possible ways to escape.

The experience helped form my opinions about whether women should be allowed to fight in combat. SERE School gave me a solid education in how men and women— including myself—respond to extremely stressful conditions.

Some people believe women shouldn't be allowed to serve in the military in certain positions, thinking they're not physically or mentally as strong as men. But in SERE School, I saw a strong male college graduate and officer almost wash out of the program because he couldn't handle the pressure of a POW training exercise. During that same exercise, an enlisted female with only her high school diploma handled everything the instructors dished out at her. She proved to be one of the toughest people I have ever met, physically as well as mentally.

I also saw firsthand in the SERE program that not everybody is cut out for combat. There are men who are and men who aren't. Likewise, there are women who are and women who aren't. Being prepared to engage the enemy takes a certain mentality that doesn't have anything to do with someone's gender.

When our training was complete, I flew home to California and went to work. In one of my most memorable exercises, I was supposed to simulate a silkworm missile attack on a ship off the coast of Southern California. The silkworm was a Chinese-made missile designed to fly low across the surface of the ocean to avoid radar detection. As the missile got close to its target, it would pop up suddenly, then come straight down on its mark.

Lisa Nowak was my friend and the electronic warfare officer, or back seater. She and I launched from Point Mugu and flew low over the waves toward our target for the day, a guided-missile destroyer. It's a big ship, though not as big as an aircraft carrier. We approached the ship from behind some islands.

Traveling at five hundred miles an

> Being prepared to engage the enemy takes a certain mentality that doesn't have anything to do with someone's gender.

hour and only two hundred feet above the ocean is a serious rush! At that low height above the water, the world races by with no room for mistakes.

At the right time, I popped up and started a steep climb to imitate the silkworm's movements. This gave the ship a chance to practice identifying and tracking us with their equipment. At somewhere around fifteen thousand feet, I rolled over and pulled the nose down to point right at the ship. I kept the jet's nose steady until I needed to pull up—and not scare the sailors or myself. Then I rose into another steep climb. As I started to pull off, I noticed a huge splash right beside the ship.

"What do you think that splash was?" Lisa asked.

"You saw it too?" I said. "Maybe they're practicing lowering lifeboats?"

She chuckled, and we set up for another run. I flew the same profile, but this time Lisa hit them with a jamming problem to solve. As I was pulling off from the second run, we both saw another huge splash beside the ship. I finally radioed the ship to ask what was causing it. The voice on the other end laughed.

"It's a whale. She's been playing beside the ship for two days now. We can't shake her!"

A whale had taken a liking to the handsome gray destroyer. Where else could you see something like that? I loved my job.

WOMEN IN COMBAT

Women have risked their lives in war throughout history. However, they often fought on unofficial terms. In the United States, the military banned women from all combat roles for most of the twentieth century. In 1948, Congress made the combat exclusion policy official. This law prevented women from fighting in any kind of combat. In 1993, the secretary of defense lifted the policy for aviators and sailors. In 2013, the ban on ground combat was lifted as well.

REVOLUTIONARY WAR | 1775–1783

- Some women disguise themselves as men to fight.
- Anna Maria Lane enlists with her husband in **1776** and fights in four battles.
- Deborah Sampson enlists as Robert Shurtleff. She is wounded in action in **1782** and digs a bullet out of her own thigh to avoid having a doctor discover her identity.

WOMEN
⋆
IN COMBAT

By the **1900s** the military requires physical examinations that prevent women from fighting in disguise.

CIVIL WAR | 1861–1865

- More than 400 women fight in the Civil War dressed as men.
- Laura J. Williams, under the name of Lt. Henry Benford, leads a company of Confederate soldiers in **1862**.
- Harriet Tubman leads Union soldiers in a nighttime raid at Combahee Ferry in **1863**, rescuing more than 700 slaves.

WORLD WAR II | **1941–1945**

- Female spies unofficially fight Nazis during secret operations. Some are captured or killed.

- **1948** Congress allows women in the military but bans them from combat roles.

FIGHT LIKE A GIRL

- **1972** Cmdr. Elizabeth Barrett commands in a combat zone during the Vietnam War.

- **1991–1992** 41,000 women deploy to combat zones during the Persian Gulf War.

- **1998** Female fighter pilots drop bombs and launch missiles in combat during Operation Desert Fox in Iraq.

- **2003–2014** 280,000 women serve in combat operations in Iraq and Afghanistan out of 2 million total service people. More than 800 of these women are wounded.

- Leigh Ann Hester receives the Silver Star for valor in combat in **2005.**

- **2011** An all-female team flies an Air Force combat mission in Afghanistan.

- **2018** Hundreds of women serve in Army combat jobs that had been previously closed:

  - infantry
  - special operators
  - fire support
  - armor

SHIFTING POLICIES

- **1993** Congress permits women to serve in aerial combat missions and on combat ships.

- **2013** The military opens some ground combat roles to women but makes more than 1,000 exceptions.

- **2015** The military opens all combat roles to women.

NO PILOT ERROR

Before flying missions in my fleet squadron, I had to learn to fly the A-7 Corsair. VA-122 in Lemoore, California, was where A-7 pilots learned to fly. Dean was already there. I was so excited to be in the same town with him again!

But my excitement was short-lived. When I arrived, I walked into the most hateful environment I had ever experienced.

Around that time, *Flying Magazine* came out with a story about female A-7 pilots. There were only a handful of us at the time, and the cover featured a photo of two of them in front of an A-7. Before a ready room full of instructors and students, including me—the only female in the squadron—the XO ripped off the cover. Then he crumpled it up, pretended to wipe his rear with it, and threw it on the ground.

"That's what I think of women flying A-7s," he said.

From then on, instructors and students avoided me. Those who went further and chose to be mean to me safely assumed their behavior wouldn't be punished.

One instructor pilot—I'll call him Black Socks— caused me the most trouble. When we briefed a flight together, he would never look me in the eyes. When a person won't look you in the eyes, something is up. In my experience, guys like the XO and Black Socks seemed to hang their egos on the fact that they were naval aviators. They didn't like the thought of a female flying their "man's" jet.

As a new student in the A-7, I flew a two-plane formation flight with Black Socks from Southern California back to Lemoore. I was the lead aircraft, and he was my *wingman*. There was a storm brewing in Lemoore, and by the time we arrived, the weather was too harsh for us to land. We entered a holding pattern to wait for conditions to calm. The winds were blowing at well over a hundred miles per hour directly across our holding pattern. I had to make constant adjustments to stay in the correct airspace.

I handled this fine until my plane's primary flight instruments died. That left me in a partial-panel condition. I had only a small backup indicator (called a peanut gyro) down by my right knee to tell me if the plane was level, and a magnetic compass to tell me which way to go. Because of the fierce winds, the compass was bouncing around so much that I could only estimate my general direction.

This was a serious emergency. I was still learning the jet, and we were soon going to be in some thick *goo*— Navy slang for flying in dense clouds. I let Black Socks know about my situation, and we switched places so he could lead.

My choice would have been to fly to a safe airport, but Black Socks decided we would land at Lemoore as planned as soon as the weather met minimum safety standards. I didn't really have a choice, but I reasoned that all I had to do was fly in tight formation under his wing. I did this and we continued to hold.

While the winds were still raging, Black Socks got a call from air traffic control. He was out of the holding airspace and at risk of getting in the way of other aircraft. He made the necessary adjustment to get back into holding. This happened twice. Considering the strong winds, I didn't fault him.

Finally, the weather improved just enough to try to land. But there were still about twenty-eight thousand feet of horrible weather between us and the earth below. We wouldn't break out of the clouds until we were just two hundred feet above the ground, where we would be met with howling winds and driving rain.

In a partial-panel situation, it's the flight lead's

responsibility to get his wingman to a place where he can see the runway and safely land. But when air traffic control asked Black Socks if we would be approaching together or separating for single approaches to the parallel runways, he surprised me. "Single," he said, then pulled away from me. Already in the goo, I immediately lost sight of him.

I was shocked and disoriented. Switching from flying formation to flying instruments when you know it's coming is confusing enough. When you don't know it's coming, and you don't have any instruments except a peanut gyro, it's hard to know which way is up.

Black Socks hadn't lined up with the runway, so I immediately told air traffic control I was partial panel and would need a no-gyro approach. That meant rather than giving me instrument headings to follow, they had to give me step-by-step directions: "Left . . . turn . . . stop turn . . . right . . . turn . . . stop turn . . ."

The air traffic controller talked me to the runway, one point at a time. Increase descent, decrease descent. Start turn, stop turn. Step-by-step, she lined me up and led me onto the glide slope. When I put my landing gear and flaps down, I also lowered the A-7's tailhook, just like the tailhook in my T-2 that caught cables on the aircraft carrier. A-7s don't handle well on wet runways, so it's standard to catch a wire if the surface has standing water.

As I headed down, my whole world was a peanut gyro and the voice of the controller. Landing almost blind in a fierce storm was a true test of my nerves. Just before it was time to decide whether to push the throttle up and make another pass, I caught sight of the runway through my rainswept windscreen.

I thought I was home free.

I followed the meatball all the way to touchdown, then hit the runway as if it were the deck of an aircraft carrier. As I crossed the cable, I felt my jet decelerate, but I didn't come to a stop. Instead the plane jerked sideways, and I found myself sliding toward the right side of the runway. At that point, my brakes were useless, and returning to the air was not an option. I was along for the ride. I ended up sunk in the mud off the side of the runway.

> Landing almost blind in a fierce storm was a true test of my nerves.

Over the next two days, my superiors held meetings. They asked questions of everyone but me. *How did this happen? Why did this happen?*

During one hearing, Black Socks insisted that I couldn't handle my aircraft. At one point he said, "Well, I knew she was a weak student when she was blown out of the holding pattern."

I did a double take. Air traffic control had called *him* on being blown out of the holding pattern.

He ended his testimony with, "She called me for the first time when she ran off the runway."

I longed to speak, but the skipper was in charge of the hearing, and he never asked my side of the story.

Dean was away on an assignment at the time, so I called and told him what was happening. He encouraged me, but he had no more authority in the squadron than I did. There was nothing he could do.

After the inquiry, the maintenance officer—a lieutenant commander with the same authority as an Ops O—called me to his office. He had been present at the hearing.

"There were a number of times during the hearing that the look on your face made me think you had something to say," he said. "I'd like to hear it."

"Sir, with all due respect, I don't know why Black Socks said those things," I said. I told him my plane was partial panel, and I had given Black Socks the lead.

"You were partial panel?" The maintenance officer hadn't heard anything about that. He advised me to go straight to maintenance control and make an entry about it in the aircraft logbook. Then he said, "If I were you, I would contact air traffic control and get a recording of their exchanges with you two. Then I would confront Black Socks. He knows what he did was wrong. That's why he's deflecting the attention to you."

This was the first conversation I'd ever had with the maintenance officer. We weren't friends, but when I left that meeting, I felt like I had someone who would stand up for me.

I never sat in on another meeting about the incident. But within days, I was back in the cockpit. Black Socks was spreading rumors about me around the squadron, but as usual, my mom and dad had wise advice: "Consider the source and move on." I took that on board, buried my head in the books, and kept flying.

I did what the maintenance officer recommended and ordered a copy of the tapes. When I finished the A-7 training and was about to go back to Point Mugu, I asked Black Socks if I could speak to him privately. He and I went into a briefing room, and I played the tape of his conversations with air traffic control during our flight.

I asked him, "Why did you say I was blown out of the holding pattern when it was you?"

He said nothing and walked out of the briefing room.

Navy investigators from outside the squadron came to investigate. They concluded there was "no pilot error," and I was cleared to continue to fly. I eventually received the award for one thousand mishap-free flying hours. I was proud of that then, but there would come a day when it would become even more meaningful.

BOMBS AWAY

My experiences in Lemoore shook me up. Why did my presence spark such open hate? What had I done to invite it? I realized that my welcome, or unwelcome, in a squadron depended on the leadership. And leadership changed every couple years.

I had to rely on the belief that my value was based solely on what God, not people, thought of me. That confidence was not automatic, however. I had to pull myself out of sad slumps by remembering to wrap my mind around that truth—not feelings. Standing on truth, I could weather the storms that continually rolled in.

Soon after I returned to Point Mugu, Commander Mariner advanced from executive officer to commanding officer of the aggressor squadron. She was the first woman to command an aviation squadron in our nation's history.

As skipper, Commander Mariner wasted no time. She secured more funding so we could fly more missions, and she molded our squadron into a well-oiled machine. She made it possible for Pam Lyons and me to obtain our A-7 weapons qualifications. Though we'd been allowed to learn to fly the jets, the strafing (shooting bullets from jets) and bombing phases were off-limits. But now, under her orders, I returned to Lemoore to complete weapons training.

I was so excited to learn these skills and to be with Dean for a couple of weeks. Little by little, Dean and I made our house our home. I decorated and sewed curtains, and he built a handsome deck out back with seating around it. We hosted a squadron party. Many days I woke up and simply thought, *I am so blessed*.

But VA-122 hadn't changed. After completing the ground school portion of our weapons training, Pam and I were scheduled for a nighttime warm-up flight. We headed out to the practice area in a three-plane formation, with our instructor in the lead A-7. Pam and I flew behind and slightly above him, one of us on each wing. Then in a surprise move that broke all kinds of night-flight safety rules, our instructor descended toward the high mountains of the Sierra Nevadas. He rolled his plane upside down before descending the other side of the ridgeline.

The instructor was using a mean-spirited dust-off maneuver to shake us out of formation. A core value of flying formation is flight integrity—you watch out for each other. The lead pilot is supposed to be watching out for his wingmen and flying like he intends to return with them.

Any pilot would have called his roll over the mountaintop a dangerous move. To remain in position, Pam and I would have had to hold our places above his wings when he rolled over, which would have put us upside down between him and the ground. Flying upside down is not a big deal in tactical aviation. But you would never put your wingmen upside down and close to the ground at any time of day, let alone in the dark. You'd never require them to pay attention to staying in formation and avoiding the ground at the same time.

In spite of our lead's stunt, our job was to follow him. Pam and I refused to be dusted off. We also rolled over and instinctively pulled in closer. But we transitioned to a safer position under his wing, keeping his plane between ours and the mountainside.

He descended the slope halfway down into a valley before rolling upright again.

While flying upside down, I wondered if our instructor had made a bet with his buddies that he could lose us. His disregard

Pam and I refused to be dusted off.

for us made me think of Black Socks's behavior on my partial-panel flight.

After we landed, the three of us all returned to the ready room. The other pilots seemed surprised to see Pam and me with the instructor. At best, they would have shamed us if we had lost our place on the instructor's wing and had to fly back alone. At worst . . . well, I try to think better of them than that.

Of course, Pam and I were still in a season when few female naval pilots existed. There were even fewer female pilots of tactical aircraft. As always, some male pilots welcomed us, and others didn't. As for those guys who didn't, I tried to win them over, as when I managed to change Captain Cornejo's opinion that women shouldn't fly.

But it didn't always happen.

Pam and I did well in strafing and bombing—so well that the officer in charge seemed to resent our performance. He decided that female pilots wouldn't be allowed to do strafing runs with bullets. It didn't matter that the male pilots used bullets and Commander Mariner had paid for Pam and me to do the same. Next he took away our bombs. I challenged this, and we were allowed to continue with bombs, but not with everyone else. We were separated from the men and only allowed to fly a couple of patterns over and over again. All of this meant that we would learn nothing new, defeating the whole point of our being there! It was a frustrating environment.

Some people were pulling for Pam and me, however—the enlisted troops. Though far in rank below the executive officer, they were far above him in good character. For example, when Pam received mail, the XO would throw it across the *hangar*. If she wanted it, she had to go gather it up off the floor. The troops started holding her mail back so they could hand it to her.

One day our flight instructor said a lot of negative things about having to fly with "the girls" on a bombing flight. After he got into his jet, the instructor couldn't see the guys on the ground checking his bombs, which were mounted on racks under his wings. But Pam and I, in jets on either side of him, could see everything. As I looked over, I saw one of the ground crew using a huge pair of pliers to bend the fins attached to our instructor's bombs. I radioed Pam.

"Go Barbie," I said. This was our code for switching to a private radio frequency so the instructor couldn't hear us. "Check out Sweetie's bombs," I told her. Sweetie was our own nickname for this instructor, not his actual call sign.

We both laughed so hard that we could hardly finish our checklists!

As the three of us taxied out, the ground crew lined up with big grins on their faces. They even did the wave like a football stadium cheer. That day our instructor didn't get a single bomb on target. He wasn't even close. The twisted fins had made his bombs zoom around in crazy directions, much like blown-up balloons when you let them go without tying off the ends.

Pam and I had to fly with Sweetie several more times. Perhaps I should say he had to fly with us. Because the ground crew was in our corner, he and the other rude instructors often slung bombs all over Southern California and nowhere near the bull's-eye. They called it "the curse of the girls."

In the end, while we weren't allowed to do exactly the same training as the men, Pam and I were allowed to fly, and we completed the bombing and strafing components in the A-7. We finished our weapons training, and we finished well.

Commander Mariner decided we should keep going. "If you're first into the jungle, you need a good machete to cut a path," she sometimes said. It didn't take long to realize what she meant. Pam and I didn't have a machete; we *were* the machete.

We were going to be among the first women to fly the F/A-18!

THE F/A-18
HORNET

It's hard to fully describe the F/A-18 Hornet to someone who has never seen one up close. It's the type of aircraft you want to get your picture taken next to when you're at an air show. The Navy's flight demonstration team, the Blue Angels, have been flying F/A-18s for more than thirty-five years. It's an incredible machine, an agile fighter and attack jet with a top speed of Mach 1.8, faster than the speed of sound (Mach 1).

In the early 1990s, the Hornet was the coolest jet in the Navy's inventory, but there were no opportunities for women to fly it. Rumors were spreading, however, that the combat ban would be lifted soon for female aviators, and Commander Mariner was one of the drivers behind that change. It made sense for her to start putting women in the places they needed to be when it finally happened (which it did in 1993).

Finally in 1991, I sat in an actual Hornet cockpit for my first flight. The jet seemed as tough from the cockpit looking out as it had from the ground looking up. The Hornet's throttles and stick were covered with buttons and switches. These allowed the pilot to do everything from fire missiles to designate targets on a cockpit computer screen, all without letting go of the controls. The edges of the cockpit were nearly as low as my elbows, and the canopy formed a glass bubble over the top. The visibility ahead and behind was greater than it had been in any other plane I'd flown.

No experience on the ground came close to flying an F/A-18. It felt better than the fastest horse ride I've ever been on while running at a flat-out gallop. I could look in any direction, and it seemed the plane would head that way. It was truly a dream to fly. I loved the challenge of organizing and taming the thousand details of flight into a tight operation of mind and motion. The Hornet was as graceful as it was deadly.

My first flight in the jet was a cross-country flight to Chicago. It felt like a dream to pilot what I had always admired but never expected to fly. In a word: it was a *blast.*

WHAT ARE THE BLUE ANGELS?

The Blue Angels are the Navy's flight exhibition team. Since forming in 1946, they have performed exciting formation flights and difficult aerial maneuvers at air shows around the world. In their tightest formation (the Diamond 360 maneuver), they fly only eighteen inches apart! Blue Angel pilots are from the Navy and Marine Corps and have a minimum 1,250 hours of tactical jet flying experience. In 2015, the Blue Angels welcomed their first female pilot, Marine Captain Katie Higgins, to the team. She flies their C-130T Hercules transport.

My initial instructor for the Hornet, Mike Frische (call sign Micro), was a superb pilot. Flying with him felt like flying with an older brother. Unfortunately, no one followed Micro's class act for quite some time. Squadron leadership continued to be annoyed at the presence of female pilots. The operations officer at the squadron where I trained—a different Ops O from the one who had made life so challenging during my jet training days—was tall and a bit stout, in his early thirties. I'll call him Ziffel.

"Women should not be in the squadron!" Ziffel said to me one day after we had finished a session in the F/A-18 simulator. "Only warriors deserve to fly this plane." It was true I hadn't been to war. But neither had he, so I thought he used the term *warriors* with a little more weight than he should. But he continued his rant against female pilots.

When he wasn't looking, I glanced at my watch. I needed to get to the squadron and prepare for a formation flight. When he finally paused, I explained why I needed to go. He just kept talking, and for a long while I held my tongue. But by the time another pause came, I needed to let him know I was running late for my next brief.

"Sir," I said, "you have the right to feel the way you do. But I would say the solution is to convey your displeasure to your congressman. Vote in such a manner that your voice is heard. By law I have the right to wear this uniform, and quite frankly, I need to get on to my next flight."

This annoyed the Ops O—truth, if we don't like it, can often have that effect. He had to fill out my grade sheet while I was present, so he eventually scowled and scrawled his way through the form. He gave me one below-average mark, then scribbled his signature and thrust the form at me. I took it and ran, making it to the squadron just in time to brief my four-plane formation flight.

That night at home, my phone rang. Dean was away, so I answered, thinking it might be him. But Ziffel's voice thundered across the line, rambling on about his hatred for me.

"I'm not going to pass you," he announced. "Women have no right to be here!" When I heard other men cheering him on in the background, I hung up.

The call upset me. In times like these, it was important to examine my own motives for flying, for sticking with it in spite of the opposition. Had I given Ziffel any reason to hate me? Did I have the skills I needed to be in the program? Was I here on real merit? The milestones I had passed and the grades in my training jacket—the folder that held records of my flights—said I was.

What were my motives for being here? Was I here for the applause? Nope—there was none. I was here because I loved my country and wanted to serve. I wanted to earn a living because I had more than my own life to

I was here because I loved my country and wanted to serve.

care about. I wanted the means to take care of my sister and my parents, who time and again had helped me. That's what families do. And, of course, I wanted to *fly*.

The next morning, when I went to the training department, I discovered that Ziffel had put a long, handwritten letter inside my training jacket. The letter went on for pages, every line a hurried scrawl. According to the letter, I was "a terrible pilot" and "a terrible person."

Training jackets can include only Navy-approved forms. But this letter was written on loose sheets of yellow paper. I wasn't sure what to do with this personal message in my official folder.

Commander Mariner had moved on from VAQ-34 by then to write high-level speeches for the chiefs of staff in Washington, DC. I called her and asked for advice.

"He probably just got stirred up when his buddies were around," she said. "Take your jacket privately to his office, remind him that only approved forms are allowed, and say you'd appreciate him removing the letter. He'll do it, because it doesn't benefit him to break policy like this." She always looked at the better side of humanity.

But when I went back to the training department to get the jacket, it had mysteriously disappeared. I visited the Ops O without it.

In his office, Ziffel frowned and wouldn't look me in the eye. I asked him to remove the letter from my jacket. Then I said, "If you want to vent about my being here, you can go up the chain of command. But my jacket needs to be about flying only."

He harrumphed and said, "I need to make a phone call. You can leave."

After I did my next flight, I went to put the form in my training jacket. But it was still missing. I continued with that day's flights, but the next day the jacket still hadn't turned up. This went on for a few days until the officer in charge of training pulled me aside. "Lieutenant Shults, I'm sorry," he said. "But we're going to have to stop your training until we can find that jacket."

I took a deep breath and said, "Don't worry. I'll track it down." I marched over to the Ops O's office and asked him where my jacket was.

"Don't bother me," he said, "I'm busy."

With no jacket, the squadron stopped my training. I called Commander Mariner again. She suggested I present the problem to the JAG officer (naval attorney). Apparently she also mentioned the issue to someone else because the next day I was called into the XO's office, where he let me have it.

"How dare you go outside the squadron to talk with anyone!" he shouted at me. "You had no right to call your old skipper! You will not call her again!"

I stood at attention with the military bearing I'd learned in AOCS while the drill instructor shouted us down. I knew how to be emotionless on the outside, free to think as I wished on the inside.

My training jacket mysteriously reappeared the next day, so my training resumed.

In those seasons that seemed so grim, with forces set against me while Dean was away, I often called my parents. My mother would listen to my complaints and agree with my feelings. Then she'd remind me: "Life may look hard right now, Tammie Jo, but tomorrow morning the sun will rise and the birds will sing. The people who are against you don't hold the order of your life in their hands. God is in control of that. And don't take any of their accusations too personally. Jesus was perfect, yet He was treated far worse. So take heart, hon. When you struggle, you're in good company."

Of course, she was right.

When I finished my F/A-18 training, I returned to Point Mugu and resumed flying aggressor missions, now in the Hornet. I continued to make simulated attacks on ships, and we also took on more air-to-air missions as *bogies*, or imitation enemies, for TOPGUN and other squadrons. I knew this opportunity wouldn't last forever, and I wanted to make the most of it. Flying the Hornet never got old. This assignment, though not a fleet squadron, wasn't a bad way to serve.

COMMERCIAL PILOT

In 1993, I sensed my time in the military was drawing to a close. I had stayed a year beyond my commitment to the Navy, but I couldn't make military life fit with my vision of a family life with kids. Dean and I both made the decision to leave the military and step into *civilian* life, one of us at a time. Dean would do a two-year tour instructing at the Strike Fighter Weapons School Pacific while I started into civilian life.

I finished my official tour of duty in March 1993. At the end of my final flight in the Hornet, I sat in the jet, in the hot pits (where pilots can refuel without shutting down the aircraft), and grabbed a pen and a piece of paper. I had to keep my hands in sight of the fuelers, so I put my paper on the glareshield, an airplane's dashboard. I wrote a note of thanks for the time I had been granted to serve my country. The note wasn't to anyone in particular. In my mind, I was talking to my husband, family, friends, and God. I was simply grateful to be born in a country I was proud to serve, one that had opened so many doors to women during my short time in the military. I sensed even more doors would open in the near future. The note, which I could have sent to so many people, rested for years in the pocket of the flight jacket I was wearing that day.

For two more years I continued to serve in the United States Naval Reserve, in a nonflying status. By the time I left the Navy for good in 1995, I'd become a lieutenant commander and had received a National Defense Service Medal, an expert pistol marksmanship medal, and twice received the Navy and Marine Corps Achievement Medal.

Do I think of myself as a trailblazer? No. My intent was not to change the military, but simply to fly in it. Only after finishing certain phases of flight training or flying certain aircraft did I realize, *Wow. I guess we did something that hasn't been done before.* Not every first is celebrated in big, public ways.

It is rare that one person can change the course of history, be that in aviation or the military or any other arena. I owe my aviation opportunities to a host of people, beginning with the men who unlocked those doors and the women ahead of me who pushed them open. If the admirals hadn't supported us, if the Commander Mariners hadn't championed us, if the Micros hadn't welcomed us, if the enlisted servicemen and women hadn't given us a hand, we would not have succeeded.

After I left the military, I spent a summer flying for a company called Serve Air, which helped fight forest fires in Southern California. The Cessna O-2 Skymaster was nothing like the Hornet, but I enjoyed the work. I flew with a forest ranger, spotted fires, communicated with other aircraft in the area, and kept an eye out for the firefighters on the ground.

My intent was not to change the military, but simply to fly in it.

Late one afternoon, a ranger and I circled over a raging fire being chased up multiple canyons by the wind. Firefighters on top of a ridgeline were surrounded on three sides by the blaze. The wind changed direction, and fingers of fire crept up the hill behind them, threatening to cut off their only escape route. They needed to evacuate *now*.

I flew in low over the group, and the ranger threw out a large, weighted bag attached to a long, red streamer. The bag was a signal alerting the firefighters to retreat immediately. Their escape route was drawn on a map inside the pouch. In case they couldn't get to the bag, I circled back around and flew over them in the only direction they could go to safety. I made one last pass to make sure they got the message. They did, and fortunately they all survived. On days like that, we saved more than architecture and land-scapes. We flew between disaster and those brave hearts on the ground who put their lives on the line every time they showed up.

As much as I enjoyed the work and the other Serve Air pilots, I knew fighting forest fires wasn't going to be a long-term job for me. Dean and I would be moving as soon as his latest tour in the Navy ended. We wanted children, but it was impossible to say when that would happen. One day, after being introduced to a pilot for Southwest Airlines, Dean and I decided I would look into becoming a *commercial airline* pilot.

HOW IS FLYING A PASSENGER AIRCRAFT DIFFERENT FROM FLYING A FIGHTER JET?

Think of a fighter jet as a fast, maneuverable race car. A commercial airliner is more like a big, heavy eighteen-wheeler truck. The larger aircraft requires more forward thinking and planning because it takes time to get something that big to change directions and altitudes. Passenger jets are powerful, heavy, and have to be respected. The smaller fighter jets can move quickly and perform more complicated maneuvers. Both fighter jets and passenger aircraft have dozens of control inputs, and they both have to be learned and mastered. The thrills of flying one are different from the benefits of the other, but pilots of both vehicles find their jobs very rewarding.

It wasn't an easy process. The competition was fierce. The Gulf War had recently ended, and military funds were being reduced. They were offering cash to encourage pilots to leave the service, so there were more pilots than usual trying for a limited number of jobs in commercial aviation. These same pilots were also competing for a limited number of slots in training schools where they could get a special license, called a 737-type rating, that Southwest required applicants to have. The training was expensive, and I needed to complete it quickly because Southwest accepted pilot applications only once a year.

Fortunately, I found a school in Los Angeles that had a slot available. I could obtain the rating in time to apply to Southwest during their next application period. But when I was close to the end of the course, the school said I couldn't finish the training, even though I had paid for it. "You are a woman and don't need a job," they told me. I couldn't believe it. I thought I'd left that mind-set behind.

"Well," I said, "I've paid for this course, so if you won't let me finish it, I'll need my money back." Fortunately, it didn't come to that, and I eventually headed back home with my 737-type rating in hand.

When Southwest started accepting pilot applications, they took *only* the first five thousand that arrived. They threw the rest in the trash. The year I applied, Southwest received more than five thousand applications on the first day!

I was one of the fortunate ones. It wasn't long before I received a call inviting me to interview in person. I flew out to Phoenix and was offered the job, then started my training in March 1994. I was one of only two hundred pilots selected from that huge pool of five thousand.

YOU'RE FIRED

When I joined Southwest Airlines, women had been flying for the company for about ten years. However, there
were still very few of us, and just like in the military, not
all the men were happy about our presence. In addition,
several events around this time fed the idea—for those
who wanted to believe it—that women in the military just
made trouble.

In 1991 at a Navy convention called Tailhook, a
female naval aviator was attacked. She accused a number of the male attendees of harming her. The Navy
formally disciplined more than three hundred male
officers—not because they had all been part of the bad
behavior but because their silence gave consent to it. The

event angered a lot of men who thought the discipline had been unfair.

Then in 1994, just months after I began flying for Southwest, naval aviator Kara Hultgreen died during a carrier landing in her F-14 Tomcat. When one of her jet's engines stalled, Kara couldn't recover and was forced to eject. Unfortunately, her jet was rolling to the side. It launched her into the ocean, and she died when she hit the water. Kara died serving her country, just as many men had before her. Still, some people used her death to support their arguments that women didn't belong in the cockpit. For some time, her tragic death and the Tailhook scandal renewed some pilots' objections to female pilots—in and out of the military.

Fortunately, the majority of Southwest captains had great attitudes. One of my very first captains, Sumner Wyall, was legendary within the Southwest pilot ranks. On my first day of flying with him, I noticed he wore a pair of silver aviator wings that had been crafted into a ring. When I asked about it, he told me the wings had belonged to his mother, who'd flown with the Women's Airforce Service Pilots (WASPs) during World War II. She had taught him to fly. Sumner was funny and lighthearted with a contagious laugh. Other captains I flew with early on were just as pleasant. They often darted off between flights and returned with treats for their new first officer. How could I not feel welcomed?

Not everyone was like that, though. I flew with a

captain who bullied everyone, men and women alike. He yelled at me in front of passengers. Many times, he threw my paperwork in the trash and poured coffee on it. Another captain talked about disgusting topics and gave me poor performance reviews when I wouldn't join in. A third captain couldn't stand me from the moment he met me, and I never learned why. On our first flight together, he pointed his finger in my face and said, "I hate you. I am not your friend. I don't want to hear anything from you unless I ask for a checklist." He ruined two of my pilot's hats, a required part of my uniform, by stomping on them. I had to fly with him for a whole month.

By the end of my first year with Southwest, I had flown with more than forty different captains. Almost all forty treated me respectfully, gave me above-average grades, and had nothing bad to say. Only these three men were rude and insulting and gave negative reports about me.

As a company, though, Southwest lived up to its positive reputation. I met terrific pilots who taught me not only how to fly a Boeing 737 but also what it means to be a good captain.

A few months after I finished my first year, I was able to switch my base to Phoenix, Arizona, a little closer to Dean in California. The first time I arrived in Phoenix, I went to introduce myself to the chief pilot and his assistant. The chief wasn't in, but his assistant chief was, so I knocked on the door of his office, and he called me in.

The first thing I noticed was an enormous painting on

the wall behind him. It was of an F-15 Eagle, the reigning fighter jet in the US Air Force at the time. Clearly, he had flown the Eagle, and this was his baby. A friendly competition exists between Eagle pilots and Hornet pilots, and I was fairly certain the assistant chief knew my background.

The assistant chief left me standing while he slouched behind his desk. Rather than return my greeting, he launched into a lecture. Nobody cared what I'd flown in the military, he said. We were all Boeing pilots at Southwest. Nobody wanted to hear about the Hornet, and it was in my best interest to keep my head down and my mouth shut.

I remained quiet and soaked in this odd welcome.

"So you think you're special," he eventually said.

I was still wondering why he'd felt the speech was necessary and had no idea where he was going. "No, sir. I don't."

"You don't think there's *anything* different about you?"

I tried to smile politely. "I guess I am a little different. In a bushel of red apples, I'm a green apple, but I'm still just an apple."

At that, the assistant chief resumed his lecture. "We're all just pilots here," he repeated. "Your past is just that— your past. No one cares."

It was hard not to compliment the desk-sized monument to his past covering the wall behind him! But when he finished and I said nothing, he shook his head and pointed toward the door. On that strange note, I left to fly my next trip.

What had triggered this chilly reception? I sure didn't know. But by this time, I knew better than to dwell on such behavior. I was only responsible for my own acts and not everyone else's. I concentrated instead on my job.

A few weeks after I started flying out of Phoenix, I was summoned to the chief pilot's office. This time the chief was there with the assistant chief. Neither of them smiled or invited me to sit.

The chief said, "Have you ever damaged an aircraft?"

"No, sir."

He asked the question again in a slightly different way.

Again I said, "No, sir."

Tag-teaming, the two of them shot off rapid-fire questions that dealt with every conceivable part of an aircraft. Had I ever put excess wear and tear on an aircraft? Had I ever damaged a tire? Had I ever cracked a windshield? Had I ever scuffed the paint?

> The chief said, "Have you ever damaged an aircraft?"

My answer was always "No, sir"—with the exception of confirming I'd experienced some flat and blown tires.

Abruptly, the assistant chief opened the door and pointed for me to leave. I asked what the questions were about, but both of them stayed as silent as stone.

A week later I was called in to another meeting. This time we were joined by a representative from the pilot's union, an organization that works to make sure commercial pilots have a fair work environment. His presence surprised me. A union rep is someone who protects employees. I hadn't asked my union to give me a representative. Why would I need one?

This meeting was almost an exact repeat of the first. The three men drilled me with the same line of questioning. Again they went over every part of a plane. Again they offered no explanation about why they were asking these questions. I thought it was strange that my union rep seemed to take the chief pilot's side. He didn't answer my own questions or act supportive.

Within a week, a friend at Southwest headquarters called me and said in a hushed voice, "Tammie Jo, they're looking at your job application. They're trying to claim you lied on it, that you don't really have a clean safety record."

Stunned, I thanked my friend and hung up. They were questioning my safety record? I'd achieved every possible safety-standard award in my naval career. Some kind of trouble was brewing, but I couldn't imagine what it was.

I called Rosemary Mariner, who had been promoted to captain. She suggested I get a lawyer. I didn't want to do that. Not yet. But when I learned that the union rep was close friends with the chief and his assistant, I called the union and spoke with someone else, Captain Len Legge. He checked around and suspected something underhanded was going on.

Little by little we drew back the curtain on this strange story. A new Southwest pilot had seen me from a distance one day and told his captain, "I know about that girl from the Navy. She crashed an A-7 once. I don't feel safe with her here."

The "crash" he was referring to was the Black Socks episode. I'd been cleared of all fault in that incident, so it wasn't credited to me. It wasn't on my safety record at all.

Had they been interested in the truth, the chief and assistant chief could have asked to see my Navy records. My training jacket and my logbooks officially showed my perfect safety record. They also could have called Captain Mariner and asked her to explain the situation. They could have requested a copy of my naval safety record, which confirmed the Navy's findings of "no pilot error."

Instead, they only called a few people from Black Socks's squadron. All of those statements conflicted with one another and were not officially recognized, but the chiefs decided to use them.

They summoned me to their office again. This time, the chief pilot accused me of lying on my application. I'd checked the box indicating I had no accidents, and he believed I didn't have a clean safety record.

I asked to show them my records.

The chief said, "We have no interest in your records. You're fired."

THE TRUTH WILL
OUTLIVE A LIE

My humiliation was profound. Some people believed I was a liar. I talked to a few people I trusted, but nobody seemed quite sure how to advise me. For weeks my head throbbed constantly, and my stomach ached. I had problems sleeping. One of my front teeth turned gray, and my doctor said the discoloration was caused by stress. More than once I broke down crying (something I rarely did) and found it nearly impossible to stop. I didn't go anywhere. I was usually home alone.

We had moved from California to Bandera, Texas, by this point. Dean had recently exited the military and was in new-hire training at Southwest. It was impossible for him to avoid all the gossip about the Navy Hornet pilot who got fired. Because at Southwest, people usually refer to each other by their first names, not everyone realized they were talking in front of him about his wife. It was a hard time for him too. As our sole moneymaker now, he needed to keep working. We never really questioned whether Dean would keep flying for the airline. We believed my firing was the decision of two dishonest men and not a problem with the entire company. Dean encouraged me over the phone, between classes and simulator exercises.

When you're depressed, it's hard to see in the dark without friends to guide you through it. The pianist from church, a rancher's wife named Pat Welch, would call in the mornings. She would let the phone ring until I answered and assured her I was up and facing the day. Our dearest neighbors, Betty Brister and Marshall Patton, had me over for coffee every day. Kandy Johnson and Arlene Fender, friends from my college days, took time off from their work in Missouri and visited me to cheer me up. My neighbors across the creek, the Tips, had me over for dinner.

During those months, I spent a lot of time reading my Bible. Over and over in the book of Psalms, King David asked God for help when his enemies attacked. I could relate because I felt like I had been under attack. A lot of these psalms became my prayers.

One morning when I woke, my head was clear. It was time to dry my tears, get up, and fight. I couldn't wallow in disappointment any longer. If I did, I'd be in danger of getting stuck in bitterness. I had a good brain, given to me by a good God. It was time to use it.

I met with lawyers Susan Barnes and Susan Kudla. After they heard my story, they said they'd take my case free of charge. They asked me what I wanted most: to sue the airline for money or get my job back? Without hesitation I answered that I wanted my job back. I wanted to be left alone to fly. Being able to have a choice gave me hope.

My lawyers went to work. First, they asked the union how they planned to help me. They told the union that if I couldn't get my job back, they would shine a spotlight on my union rep's failure to defend me. This approach set the union in motion. We never heard from my original rep again, but the wise and clever Captain Legge took over the preparation for my defense.

At first the chief pilot refused to give me a chance to prove my safety record. But in due time, and thanks to Captain Legge's persistence, I presented my case to four company representatives. Two of them were chosen by the union and two by Southwest. All four were pilots.

During this time, Captain Nancy Bruce became my champion. Nancy prayed with me, listened to me, and helped me shine a light on the facts rather than the emotions. She showed me how to avoid the things that would waste my time and energy. In addition to my legal team, I owe Nancy my job.

I gathered all my documents, and people who knew the truth came to my aid as well. Captain Mariner flew out from Washington, DC, to testify. I asked Captain Tom Vaughn for a written statement in my defense. Tom had been the skipper in Lemoore and was familiar with the Black Socks incident. But when he heard the details of my situation, he said, "The truth needs to be told. I'm going to fly in and testify in person."

On the day of the hearing, about twenty people gathered in front of the four pilot jurors. Southwest brought its lawyers, and several executives were present. The chief pilots who had fired me came, as did the people supporting me. The man who originally accused me of crashing an A-7, who had started this whole ugly storm, didn't show.

One Navy pilot had agreed to testify against me. He'd been a lieutenant commander in my aggressor squadron. He submitted a report before the hearing, so when he was asked to testify, he simply said, "Everything is in my report."

"The truth needs to be told."

Captain Legge picked up the paper. "Okay," he said. "Let's go over it statement by statement because Captain Mariner is here today. She was your commanding officer at the time, as well as Lieutenant Shults's, and she's familiar with all the details of the situation."

Captain Legge read the report one accusation at a

time. In front of the whole room, the lieutenant commander had to admit every charge was false. Captain Mariner never had to say a word.

The hearing dragged on for two days. At the end of the testimonies, the jury agreed I had not lied on my application. I was a safe pilot and had always been a safe pilot. They immediately gave me my job back.

The decision was rewarding at first, but in the coming days it began to feel hollow. I was exhausted. Six months had passed since I was fired, and I didn't receive lost wages or even an apology. Southwest simply gave me a few days to consider whether I wanted to return.

I wasn't sure I did.

The stress had ground me down. My reputation had been dragged through the mud. Though I'd been cleared, people would hold long memories of the accusations, even though they were false. Above all, I still couldn't explain why the chiefs had targeted me. How could I know it wouldn't happen again?

Do I really want that job back? I wondered. *Do I really want to fly for Southwest?*

Captain Mariner helped me answer the question. She called one day to see how I was doing and whether I'd made a decision. I told her why I was wavering.

"No matter what you choose, you won't be happy for a while," she said. She was right. If I went back to work, I'd still have to deal with gossiping people who didn't like me. If I quit flying, I'd truly miss it.

She continued, "Some decisions aren't a matter of happiness. Ask yourself this: When you look down the road five to ten years from now, what decision will you wish you had made? The truth will outlive a lie, Tammie Jo. It may take a while, even a long while, but truth will win in the end. And the people who don't like you don't get to determine your happiness."

Our conversation changed the way I thought about my choices.

Dean and I would start a family someday. We'd continue to live a happy life whether I took my job back or not. As a couple, the two of us were so much more than what we did for a living.

I considered my family. Dad would be retiring soon from his work as a diesel mechanic, and I wanted to do my part to care for Sandra. Families take care of each other; that's what families are for. This job would help me do that.

I called Southwest and took my job back.

My friend Captain Jim Rice arranged to fly with me on my first flight after I returned. As we boarded the plane, he said, "Forget about all this, Tammie Jo. Let's go fly and have some fun."

So we did. Everyone needs a Jim Rice in their life.

Every now and again, I saw the chief pilots who had fired me, but not often. Years later I found out they had a regular practice of "investigating" the people who worked under them, men and women, without cause. The saying

I had learned as a kid held true: bullies are never bullies to just one person. Eventually these two grown bullies' school-bus ride came to an end, and both of them were removed from management.

The first officer, now a captain, who claimed I crashed an A-7 is still around today. After all these years I've never met him, and while I cannot forget, I can forgive.

Captain Mariner was right. The truth did outlive the lie, though the process took a long time. Five years later, at the age of thirty-nine, I upgraded to captain, a position I've held for almost two decades. I love my job, and I love my company.

I made the right choice.

With this battle finally behind us, Dean and I focused on starting the family we had longed for. It seemed we might not have children of our own, so we looked into adopting.

I was away from home, out for a run, when Dean called one day. He told me about a young lady who needed a home for her unborn baby. I slowed to a walk. Were we interested in adopting her child? he asked me.

I stopped and looked up at the bright-blue sky. "Thank You, Lord!" I said out loud.

We had four months to get ready, but life began to move fast. We had so much paperwork to complete! State officials inspected our house. We were fingerprinted and background checked and certified in *CPR* (a way to restart someone's breath or heartbeat). We painted the nursery, bought a car seat and a stroller, and selected a crib.

In March 1998, we got the call we'd been waiting for and headed to the hospital. Twenty minutes after Sydney was born, her birth mother handed the tiny girl to me and said, "She needs you more than she needs me." These selfless words still fill me with gratitude.

I took three months off work to welcome this tiny baby, *our* baby, to the world. Being a parent was the most incredible thing I'd ever done. Sometimes in the mornings Dean and I would go in together to wake her up. She always smiled right away when she opened her eyes.

Dean and I had talked about me becoming a full-time mom, but I also had the option to fly a reduced schedule. The more we discussed it, the more that made sense. It can be difficult to spend a few years away from flying, then come back. In aviation, when you step out of flying, you have to start over in many ways when you return. We decided I would fly less, have more time at home, and study to stay current with technology, aircraft, and policies. So I returned to work. Life became a happy whirlwind of activity and love.

When Sydney turned fourteen months old, Dean and I began the process to adopt a second child. But then I started feeling unwell. I was tired and sick to my stomach.

> Life became a happy whirlwind of activity and love.

Usually I ran a four-mile loop each morning, but suddenly I could hardly walk a mile.

It turned out that I was pregnant!

Dean and I were so excited. But we made a pact not to tell anyone right away.

One day soon afterward, a preschooler boarded my plane. He was too frightened to walk down the aisle to his seat, so his father encouraged him to have a peek in the cockpit. After the little boy saw our captain, Captain Johnson, he caught sight of me.

"Look!" the boy told his dad. "He's flying with his mama!" The airplane had a mommy in the cockpit—that's all this little guy needed to know. He went to his seat reassured.

The next time I visited the pilots' lounge, Dean was already there. When I walked in, my colleagues shouted, "Hi, Mama!" I thought Dean had told our secret. He wildly shook his head as if to say, *I didn't!* Then Captain Johnson, several years my senior, came into view with a twinkle in his eye.

"Ready to go flying, Mom?" he asked me. Dean was innocent.

I flew for two and a half more months before taking time off until our son was born. I enjoyed being home, though I was constantly exhausted and sick. Nothing seemed to settle my stomach during the pregnancy. Yet the sheer wonder of a life forming within me eclipsed everything else. Feeling that first flutter and kick inside me took my breath away. My heart was happy, simply happy, and I often found myself singing around the house. There is something miraculous about new life.

We named our son Marshall after our retired neighbor who, with his wife, Betty, had been so kind to us and become such a good friend. When Sydney saw Marshall for the first time through the glass of the nursery window, she pointed at her new baby brother with a grin and said, "Mine? Mine!"

At that time, I was based in Houston as a senior first officer for Southwest. During the next few months, I often studied for my upgrade to captain during the night while I nursed Marshall. Sydney sometimes got out of bed and found me up with my books. She would grab her own book and join me at the breakfast table to "study." Before Marshall turned one year old, I became a captain.

In those early years, I flew about two days a week. Still, Dean's and my schedules sometimes overlapped. About four or five nights a month, we'd be gone from home at the same time. On these nights, dear friends acted as our in-home childcare.

Life took on a busy pace, and the years flew by.

Our family went on camping trips and holidays and attended plays and practices and games and recitals. We attended the T Bar M family camps in Texas every year from the time Marshall was a baby until the kids were grown and making their own adventures. We never did get to Disneyland or Six Flags, opting instead for hiking and deep-sea fishing in Alaska, snorkeling in the Bahamas, and making numerous trips to New Mexico to see Mommy and Daddy Bopa and Aunt Sandra. My ranching parents had given me animals and room to run. Dean and I gave our kids the thrill of traveling.

At home, I taught the kids reading, writing, and math. Dean taught them to ride dirt bikes, to repair things around the house, and to fish and hunt. Sydney was the first to shoot a deer. They both learned how to skin and process an animal so we could use the meat.

Over the years, our family found a peaceful stride in the midst of ups and downs. Sydney graduated from high school and started working. Marshall, a senior, was a few weeks away from graduating when I had my toughest day at work.

22

FLIGHT 1380

The morning of April 17, 2018, I awoke in my hotel room in Nashville, Tennessee, at 3:00 a.m. It was day two of a three-day trip, and I was about to fly from Nashville to New York City, then to Dallas. The morning began as usual with a cup of tea and my Bible. I always text a portion of what I've read to my family members as I pray over each of them and whatever they might be doing that day. Then, as I have ever since I became a pilot, I pray over my flights. I ask God to guide my judgment and airmanship. When I started flying for Southwest, I also started praying for my crew and passengers.

When my teacup was empty and my prayers were finished, I put on some music and got ready to go to work.

By 4:00 a.m. I was in the hotel lobby, meeting my first officer, Darren Ellisor, so we could head to the airport.

I had met Darren the day before in Houston's Hobby Airport, where we started the trip. Dean and I agree that we might have terrible weather, people drama, mechanical trouble, or delays, but if we have a good copilot, we have a good day. If the *cabin* crew has the same sunny outlook, it's a great day. When I met Darren, a former Air Force pilot, I thought, *I'm in for some good days.*

At the airport I picked up coffee for our crew, then met our flight attendants: Rachel Fernheimer, Seanique Mallory, and Kathryn Sandoval. We all put our things away, checked equipment, then stood in the forward *galley* for a short meeting.

It's common for pilots to have different flight attendants every day. The trick for me is figuring out how to quickly turn five strangers into a team. For this reason, it's my policy to make the captain's briefing about more than the weather. I try to give the team the important information quickly so we have time for more personal conversations too.

That day I learned that Rachel thought she and I had flown together once before, but neither of us was sure. Kathryn had been with Southwest for just six weeks. And Seanique had worked as a customer-service agent for a few years before becoming a flight attendant. I could tell that the women who would be assisting passengers of Flight 1380 genuinely enjoyed their jobs. Darren told us about his son's Cub Scout troop, which he leads. He and I discovered we both had seniors in high school. We joked about how hard it can be to find the right graduation gift for a senior. When I mentioned I was handwriting the book of Proverbs as a gift for Marshall, I discovered some of us shared a common faith.

I remember thinking, *This is a group I'd like to have dinner with*. It was going to be a great day!

Our trip from Tennessee to New York went smoothly. In New York, we welcomed 144 passengers to the next leg of our flight to Dallas.

At 10:27 a.m., Darren and I pushed back from the gate and started the engines. I taxied, and Darren had the radios. But it was Darren's turn to fly, so when we received clearance to take off, he took the controls. As Darren flew, I talked with air traffic control. As always, when we reached ten thousand feet, I rang the flight attendants. Everything was normal as we climbed to our cruising altitude at thirty-eight thousand feet, headed west-southwest toward Texas.

We had been airborne for about twenty minutes when it felt like a huge truck hit my side of the aircraft. My first thought was that we'd collided with another plane. Darren and I both grabbed the controls as the airplane tried to flip over on its left side. We watched as the left-engine instruments flashed and wound down. We had an engine failure.

A moment later, we couldn't see *anything*. Oxygen

masks and fire gloves went flying from their storage compartments. They bounced around in the cockpit with other loose items. The aircraft began to shudder so violently that we couldn't focus our eyes. My side of the cockpit filled with smoke, which made me think there was a fire. But the fire alarm wasn't ringing. It was like being inside a smoky snow globe that someone was shaking *hard*.

Just as suddenly, a deafening roar enveloped us. We couldn't see, we couldn't breathe, and a piercing pain stabbed our ears. In that same moment, the aircraft lurched and rolled hard to the left. The nose of the aircraft pitched over, diving toward the ground.

None of us understood what had happened until much later. The initial feeling of being hit by a truck was brought on when a piece of a turbine fan blade in the left engine snapped off. The break damaged the engine so badly that it exploded. This blast ripped off the front edge of the *cowling* (the frame that surrounds the engine) and scattered the pieces over miles of Pennsylvania. The rest of the cowling rolled back like a banana peel and flopped around in the wind. Torn pieces of the plane took chunks out of the wing and tail, ripped a panel open underneath the wing, and poked a hole in hydraulic lines around the engine. A fuel line was also cut above the shut-off valves, so we had no way of stopping fuel from

The nose of the aircraft pitched over, diving toward the ground.

flowing out of the left fuel tank. What was once a sleek and aerodynamic plane was now more like a barn door swinging in a hurricane.

Even worse, a piece of debris hit the window at row 14 and broke it. This hole in the plane generated the deafening roar and the sudden loss of air pressure. If you've ever been in a car when someone rolls down the window on the freeway, you know the noise is unpleasant. I don't have words to fully describe the ear-beating punishment of a five-hundred-mile-per-hour noise.

When the airplane's window broke, it was like popping a balloon. All of the high-pressure air rushed out of the aircraft to equalize with the low pressure of the outside air at that altitude. The sudden shift caused the piercing pain in our ears and necks. Though we practice the emergency procedures for rapid *depressurization* in the flight simulator, we can't practice its effects on the body. Air left our lungs as fast as it left the airplane. And until we could get our oxygen masks on, we were gasping for our next breath.

The damage on the left side of the aircraft caused the violent shuddering. Instead of an engine under the left wing pushing us forward, we now had what amounted to an anchor weighing us down. It felt like we were flying through an asteroid belt, hitting most of the rocks as we went. The huge difference in *thrust* between the damaged left wing and the right wing, with a working engine, pushed the nose of the aircraft to the left. That rotation caused the good wing to generate more lift than the bad wing, which made the aircraft roll rapidly toward the failed engine and dropping left wing.

Darren and I tried shouting at each other but couldn't hear a word, so we used hand signals. We had about sixty seconds to make some important decisions before our bodies had too little oxygen to function correctly. Working together, we stopped the rolling and pulled the nose around with our rudder pedals. It was Darren's turn to fly, so after he got his oxygen mask on, I nodded and took my hands off the controls to acknowledge he would still be the pilot flying.

As I put on my own mask, I recalled my days as an out-of-control flight instructor. I knew we had to work *with* this plane, not against it. In the thin air of high altitudes, massive 737s are not designed to be yanked and banked like an agile Hornet. The plane wanted to descend, so Darren and I let it. Some of the passengers later described it as being in a free fall, and I can understand how it felt like that. In the first five minutes after the explosion, we descended at a rate of almost 3,800 feet per minute, for a total of 18,900 feet. While that was much faster than a normal descent of about 2,000 feet per minute, it was not out of control.

Darren and I needed to slow the plane to reduce the shuddering and shaking. We needed to be able to focus our eyes on our instruments and checklists. We also had to decide where we could land. Darren pointed out Philadelphia on his map. It was a great option, with long runways and first responders at the field. Besides that, it was a familiar airport to both of us.

I radioed air traffic control and explained our situation. At first I told them that I thought we had an engine fire. But I realized the smoke had cleared and there was no other sign of a fire, so I revised my information.

"Okay," air traffic control said to me. "You are single engine, cleared to Philly. Can you maintain eleven thousand [feet]?"

"Yes, sir," I said.

He gave the clearance. "Southwest 1380, descend and maintain eleven thousand."

Throughout the descent, whenever we made a left turn toward Philadelphia, the aircraft wanted to roll over on the left side. Our risk of flipping over was high, but Darren did a great job of keeping control of the aircraft.

With the situation in the cockpit somewhat in hand, I turned my attention to the cabin. Only a few minutes had passed since the explosion, but a few minutes can seem like an eternity to people in a life-threatening situation.

Before I pushed the flight attendant call button, I made a cabin announcement. I doubted that anyone would hear it over the roar of air. But fortunately, many people *did* hear me—including Rachel, Seanique, and Kathryn, who couldn't hear me over the intercom. I offered everyone a simple message of hope:

"We are not going down," I said. "We are going to Philly."

Albany

Ithaca

NEW YORK

PENNSYLVANIA

Scranton

LaGuardia
Airport

Path of diverted
Southwest Flight 1380

⚠ ⚠

⚠

New York

Harrisburg

Allentown

Philadelphia

NEW
JERSEY

MARYLAND

Philadelphia
International
Airport

Baltimore

DELAWARE

Ocean
City

FLIGHT
1380
PATH

CRISIS IN THE CABIN

As chaotic as things were in the cockpit, they were worse in the cabin. The plane continued its bone-jarring shudder. Jolted passengers screamed, cried, prayed, held hands, and sent messages to loved ones on the ground. The roaring noise continued. Oxygen masks dangled from the overhead compartments, but very few people wore them correctly.

Seanique, Rachel, and Kathryn strapped on their portable oxygen bottles, put on the masks, and unbuckled from their *jump seats*. They began to reassure passengers and help them secure their oxygen masks.

These women weren't just doing their jobs by getting out of their seats. They were placing their own lives at risk, and no one would have blamed them for staying buckled in. But all three women *chose* to get up. The rapid depressurization told them there must be a hole in the aircraft somewhere, although they didn't know where at first. They knew that at any moment, some other part of the aircraft might tear away and suck them out of the plane.

As they stumbled down the aisle, flying debris struck them. They strained their backs and bruised their ribs as they bounced off the seats. The oxygen bottle straps cut their necks. Everyone on board had been affected by the rapid depressurization just as Darren and I had been. The crew and passengers had shooting pain in their ears and the terrifying feeling of not being able to breathe. But the attendants made their way from seat to seat, shouting over the racket while they paused to help people. "We're going to be okay! We're going to Philly!" they yelled.

Passengers later shared how that simple message changed the attitude inside the aircraft. They were still worried, but the panic began to melt away. Terror was replaced with possibility. We were still in a crippled aircraft hurtling through the sky, but now everyone knew Darren and I had control and were trying to get everyone safely on the ground.

Rachel was the first flight attendant to arrive in row 14, where rubble from the engine explosion had broken the window. When it blew out, the force had pulled the window-seat passenger's upper body out the opening. Her seatbelt kept her anchored inside.

Hollie Mackey, who had been sitting in the aisle seat of row 14, switched places with a fifteen-year-old girl in the middle seat. Hollie grabbed the woman's belt loops to attempt to pull her back in. But the pull of the rushing air outside the cabin was too great. Rachel crouched in the floor space in front of them and wrapped her arms around the window-seat passenger's thighs and pulled.

In row 15, Tim McGinty tore off his oxygen mask and seatbelt and leaned over the seats to help. Andrew Needum, a firefighter and emergency medical technician, joined the effort. He stretched across the laps of the two ladies. Someone in the aisle held his ankles, and Andrew put all of his weight into pulling on the woman, but he couldn't get her back in from that position. It seemed like a hopeless situation.

Andrew stood up. Then he yelled to Hollie and the young lady, "I'm sorry, but you're going to have to move!"

Rachel took the two female passengers up the shaking aisle to her and Seanique's jump seats in the front of the aircraft. She strapped them in while Andrew and Tim tried again. This time Andrew positioned himself in front of the woman. Both men pulled, but the force of the airflow outside the plane was working against them. Andrew slid his arm out through

It seemed like a hopeless situation.

the window hoping to grab the passenger's shoulder. The power of the wind was unbearably cold but also instantly pinned his arm. The men weren't making any progress, but they determined not to give up.

Seanique contacted Darren and me over the intercom. By this time I had taken over the controls, because it's the captain's responsibility to land the plane in an emergency. Seanique told us what had happened to the passenger in row 14. We had slowed to about three hundred miles per hour, but we needed to slow down even more to reduce the force of air rushing past the window so they could pull the woman back inside. It was the first time Darren and I understood what had caused the rapid depressurization.

In the cabin, Andrew and Tim could feel us slow down. Finally, they got the passenger back in. She was unconscious. Andrew unbuckled her seatbelt and laid her across the row of seats. Then he felt for a pulse as Seanique put out a call for anyone who knew CPR.

A retired school nurse named Peggy Phillips was on board. Peggy knew CPR and had also been trained in crisis management. When the call came for help, she got out of her seat. Peggy and Andrew performed CPR on the unconscious passenger while Rachel retrieved the emergency medical kit.

Back in the cockpit, I had my hands full. I maintained control of the aircraft and communicated with air traffic control. Darren helped me with radio frequency changes, checked and shut down the damaged systems, and stayed available to the flight attendants. Our reduced speed minimized the aircraft's shudder enough for us to focus on our instruments. The noise lessened slightly too.

As we descended below ten thousand feet, we were able to take off our oxygen masks. But we still had trouble hearing the flight attendants over the intercom.

Darren and I had a number of emergency-procedure checklists that we needed to run: There was the rapid-depressurization checklist, the engine severe-damage checklist, and the emergency-descent checklist. The hydraulic system associated with our left engine was damaged, and we had a fuel leak. Each of these situations had their own checklists too. We needed to do the single-engine descent checklist, the single-engine approach checklist, and finally, when configured for landing, the single-engine-before-landing checklist.

All of these checklists are meant to be run with both pilots involved. But that turned out to be impossible. Air traffic control had a lot of questions and put us through numerous frequency changes. Darren was also trying to give Kathryn, Seanique, and Rachel as much information as he could.

"Southwest 1380, I need fuel remaining and souls on board," a controller said to me.

"One hundred and forty-nine souls on board," I said. "Five-plus hours of fuel." In spite of our severed fuel lines, we would be landing nearly ten thousand pounds overweight, still carrying most of the fuel we should have burned on the way to Dallas.

"Southwest 1380, you gonna go right in, or do you need extended final?"

"Extended final," I said. Darren had asked for more time to get all those checklists done. We heard a considerable amount of radio chatter as the controller moved other aircraft out of our way. Then we were cleared to descend to four thousand feet.

As I began the approach, I asked the controller to have a medical team meet us on the runway. "We've got injured passengers," I said.

"Injured passengers, okay. And is your airplane on fire?"

"No," I said. "But part of it is missing. They said there's a hole and, uh"—I wasn't exactly sure how to relay this information—"someone went out."

The controller seemed caught off guard by this news. After a brief pause he said, "I'm sorry. You said there's a hole and somebody went out?"

Darren and I looked at each other and shook our heads; it was too complicated for a radio call. I focused on flying. There was nothing more to add, and I couldn't allow myself to get sidetracked by the thought of the grave situation in the cabin. I had to fly the airplane.

"Southwest 1380, we'll work it out," he said. "The airport is just off to your right. Report it in sight, please."

A few seconds later I saw it. "In sight," I said.

He cleared us for a runway and then handed us off to another controller.

I had special concerns about how we were going to land. I needed to set the wings' flaps to enable us to slow down for landing. But the deceleration caused by the typical flap setting for a single-engine failure might create too much *drag* for our severely damaged wing to handle. And that might slow us down too much, too fast.

The extra fuel we were carrying would only slow us down more. If I came in too slow, I might not reach the runway. But if I tried to keep our airspeed steady by adding power from the right engine, it would be difficult to keep the airplane level and pointed in the right direction. I couldn't add too much power, or the airplane would be pushed to fly sideways and would descend even faster. I gave Darren instructions to set our flaps at a conservative position so we could keep as much speed as possible.

At that moment, Seanique called to say the medical situation with our hurt passenger was serious. We needed to get on the ground as quickly as we could. We would not have time for a long approach and checklists. Darren told her we were moments from landing. We would just have to focus on the checklist items that were absolutely required for safety.

The tower controller told us we were cleared to land.

I needed to make one more big right turn to get us lined up with the runway. But when I put in the controls to make the turn, nothing happened.

There was a brief moment of silence on the radio as well as in the cockpit. Darren was heads down in the cockpit dialing in frequencies.

"Heavenly Father?" I said. I thought I was having a

private conversation with God. I didn't realize I'd said it aloud, but this portion of my question is on the cockpit voice recorder. The other part is not: "What am I missing?"

The answer to my problem was the same as the problem itself: the right engine. That healthy right engine was putting out too much thrust to allow me to turn right. Although I was already losing airspeed, I would have to pull power off of the right engine to be able to turn toward the runway. It was the last thing I wanted to do. I was already coming in too slow and descending too fast. But I didn't have a choice.

To reduce the engine's power, I eased the right throttle back. I turned right using my *ailerons* (on the wing) and my rudder (on the tail). It worked! As the nose slowly swung around to the right, I called for landing gear down.

We were getting close, but we weren't there yet.

IS IT SAFE TO FLY?

Yes! Flying is the safest mode of mass transportation in the world. And it's only getting safer, thanks to advancing safety procedures and improving technology. In the 1950s, deadly plane accidents happened about once every two hundred thousand flights in the United States. Now they happen only once every two million flights. You're more likely to get struck by lightning than killed in an airplane accident. Tragic accidents get a lot of attention on the news, but that's because they are so rare.

IS IT SAFE TO FLY?

- Flying on a commercial plane is the safest way to travel. It is even safer than walking.

- Air travel has the most safety regulations of any form of transportation.

- Planes are...

336 times safer than cars

6 times safer than trains

6 times safer than boats

47 times safer than bicycles

5 times safer than school buses

RELIEF AND GRIEF

I had only one shot at landing. There would be no second chance, no missed approach, no go-around. Darren and I did the before-landing checklist to be sure the gear, flaps, and speedbrakes were in the proper positions. I could see that the fire trucks were at the far end of the runway, so I intended to let the aircraft roll down to them. We needed to get medical help on board as quickly as possible.

Andrew and Peggy were still doing CPR on the passenger from row 14. As the flight attendants saw the ground whipping by the windows much faster than normal, they instructed the passengers to get in the position for an emergency landing. We had not instructed them to do this, but they didn't take any chances.

"Heads down! Stay down! Brace! Brace! Brace!"

The flight attendants stayed in the aisle without seat-belts, having given up their jump seats to the displaced passengers.

At 11:23 a.m., we touched down. It had been twenty minutes since the explosion.

"Nice Air Force landing," Darren would tease me later.

As we rolled out, the cockpit voice recorder captured me saying, "Thank You, Lord. Thank You, thank You, Lord."

Yet I knew there was still a terrible situation in the cabin.

We taxied quickly to the end of the runway. Then I steered the plane off to where a circle of fire trucks and paramedics waited. Fuel and hydraulic fluid continued to leak, and firefighters sprayed down the area.

I called back to the flight attendants and asked if they saw any smoke or fire outside. They didn't. I told them to put up the girt bars, which would prevent the emergency-exit slides from deploying when the aircraft doors opened. I wanted passengers to use airstairs instead, which are safer, but ground crews needed to bring the stairs to the plane. With six exit doors and only three flight attend-ants, passengers could have gone out a door early if they wanted to, possibly injuring themselves.

I shut down the right engine, and Darren and I went over the shutdown checklist. As soon as we were done,

I headed back to check on the flight attendants and passengers.

When I unlocked the cockpit door and stepped through, I could not have been more surprised. Instead of finding a group of frightened, anxious, and angry passengers, I was met with calm, attentive people.

At this point there were a few people in the forward galley. Rachel and Seanique were there, with debris stuck in their windblown hair. (Kathryn was in the rear section of the aircraft.) Others—who I would learn later included Andrew and Tim, some paramedics, and the FBI—were also there. It was a bit crowded.

Someone said, "Where did you come from?" My hair was not windblown like the flight attendants', and no one had seen me offering any help during the flight. (I can't help but be flattered when I'm mistaken for a flight attendant.)

Someone else said, "I'd like to shake the hand of the guy who landed this bird!"

"I landed this bird," I said good-naturedly as I reached for the PA to speak to the passengers.

"Thank you for your patience," I said to them. "I am sorry. I know this was a rough ride. God is good, and we are on the ground. Thank you for staying seated while we take care of our medical emergency first. There are stairs on the way."

"God is good, and we are on the ground."

Paramedics, firefighters, FBI agents, and mechanics had climbed an extension ladder to board the plane. The paramedics quickly took charge of our injured passenger. They used a sturdy canvas transporter called a mega mover to deliver her to the medical team on the ground. The FBI agents were there to determine if the explosion was an act of terrorism. They concluded that it was not.

I asked the flight attendants to give the passengers water, but they'd already begun. All three women could barely speak. Their throats were raw from shouting, but there they were, still continuing to serve others.

I started to move through the cabin, taking time to speak to each person and listen to their questions. I usually walk down the aisle of the aircraft if we have a lengthy delay or have had something out of the ordinary happen. We all handle life better when our questions get answers.

A baby girl slept soundly on her mother's lap. When I asked about her, her mom calmly replied that she was fine.

I remember the brave face of Andrew's young daughter. We spoke about the doll she was holding, who was also "fine."

I continued through the plane, asking each person if he or she was okay, listening, and answering questions to the best of my ability. Throughout this time, a part of my mind was always on the passenger who *wasn't* okay.

All was quiet as I returned up the aisle.

When the airstairs arrived, I helped people with their bags and gave them a hug or a high five as they exited.

In return I received nothing but expressions of politeness, courtesy, and gratitude, as well as relief.

When all the passengers were safely off the plane, I took a moment to close my eyes and offer a prayer of thanks.

I went back into the cockpit and started pulling my things together. I packed up my headset and flight bag and stowed my oxygen mask. Darren had taken care of everything else. I collected my bags and set them aside, then pulled out my phone to text my family.

I snapped a picture of the left engine, with its shredded cowling. I sent it to Dean with this line of text: "Single-engine landing in Philly."

"Your aircraft?" he texted back.

"I wouldn't claim it as mine," I wrote. "But I did fly it."

Everyone in my family responded as I would have guessed. Sydney said, "Mom, I love you. I'm so glad you're okay." Marshall quipped, "There's a reason Southwest gives you two engines." He was in class at the time, transmitting in the blind—aviation slang for not having any idea what is going on. He thought I had taken a bird in the engine and turned around to land.

Darren and I walked out of Flight 1380 together and down the stairs into the waiting medical van. He went with one emergency medical technician while I went with another. The EMT took my pulse. He looked up at me.

"How do you get through security with those nerves of steel?"

"Pardon me?" I said, pulling my wandering thoughts back to him.

"You don't even have an elevated heart rate!" he said. "You're completely calm." He rechecked my stats.

Although I'd like to take credit for such nerves of steel, I'm as human as the next person. I believe my calm voice and pulse rate that day were the product of more than my training and demeanor. They didn't magically appear in a sudden moment of need. They'd developed over the years, nurtured through each life experience as well as through my faith and confidence in God's goodness. I believe the Creator put "nerves of steel" in many people on Flight 1380 that day.

But the survival of many can never mask the loss of one. Though we returned 148 people to their lives and loved ones, my crew and I were not able to do that for Jennifer Riordan, who died of her injuries. The loss of this young woman will always weigh heavy on my heart, my crew's hearts, and my company's heart.

That evening Dean called to encourage me. For thirty years, my husband has been my best friend and favorite pilot, and his presence in my life has given me an almost unfair advantage. He understands everything about my job and can almost see my world from behind my own eyes. After the flight, Dean helped me find the words to express the confusion within myself, so I could sort it out and eventually get through it.

Dean reminded me that it's possible to grieve and

rejoice at the same time. He pointed me to a beautiful poem we both love from the book of Ecclesiastes:

> There is a time to weep and a time to laugh,
> A time to mourn and a time to dance.

April 17, 2018, was the day I fully understood those words.

HABITS, HOPE, AND HEROES

When I was a kid on the ranch, horses, hogs, and steers sometimes got the best of me, threw me off, or pushed past me. When that happened, Dad would give me a knowing nod that meant, "Go get 'em." No matter how upset I was, I had to bring back the offender, get back in the saddle, or put the outlaw back in its proper pen. I grew up thinking the reason for that was to teach the animal a lesson: crime doesn't pay.

It turned out the lesson wasn't for them at all. The lesson was for me.

I went back to work as a Southwest captain in May, only three and a half weeks after the incident on Flight 1380.

Things in life will often throw us down, slip out of our grasp, or push us aside. What is the best way to handle these experiences? "Go get 'em" echoes in my mind. In my life, both on the ground and in the air, all the things that went wrong gave me a chance to work through problems and make decisions drawing from what I had studied, learned, or experienced. Of course nobody likes problems, but those difficult times seasoned me, groomed me, and prepared me for the day I needed to fly and land Flight 1380.

That flight itself was a challenge that taught me three important lessons I will carry with me into whatever is next.

First, habits—good and bad—become instincts under pressure. In other words, the choices we make every day become our reflexes on bad days. We have the gift of choice and reason, which means we get to choose the way we behave. We can decide to regularly do things like asking questions when we don't understand something, being kind to new kids at school or in the neighborhood, or taking a deep breath or two before reacting to something that makes us mad.

Every morning when I get up, I feed the animals in our home before I make food for myself. This was something my parents taught me to do on the ranch, and it's a habit I passed on to my kids. It's a way of caring for others first, a way of starting each day with a clear mind that isn't wrapped around *me*.

Good habits are a personal gold mine and should be guarded. The reverse is also true: bad habits, which we all have, can become an anchor wrapped around our feet, dragging us down. Habits of all kinds *can* direct our behavior every day when we let them. They *will* direct our behavior in a crisis. If you have ever played a sport or a musical instrument, you've heard the saying, "You will play like you practice." It's that simple.

In a crisis, your body produces the hormone *adrenaline* to help you think clearly, but the rush it brings won't add to what you know. You'll have to depend on what you've already developed and learned.

My habit of spending daily time with a God who loves me gave me unusual peace as our plane shook and rolled. I wondered if that was the day I would meet my Maker face-to-face. I wasn't afraid, though, because I wouldn't be meeting a stranger. The peace that followed that speeding train of thought was the source of my calm while we shuddered and shook all the way down.

A number of other habits served my crew and me well that day. The few minutes we had together before the flight, talking about things that were important to us, created a foundation of trust that we needed. The habits I had developed over years of flying and training in aviation emergencies and out-of-control flights gave me a particular advantage. Darren and I already knew how to prioritize what needed our attention and when. So did our flight attendants. If we had had to stop and think through every task, we wouldn't have accomplished our job that day.

Our habits come out of what we believe about what is right and important. I believe in the value of every human being. I believe that all people are important, even if I don't know their names. This affects the way I treat others. It's why I developed the habit of walking through the cabin and speaking to each passenger when trouble has occurred. Interestingly, I've received far more interest in the way I treated my passengers after we landed than in how I got that damaged plane on the ground. This speaks to how much all of us need to feel that someone cares about us. Kindness matters.

The second truth I've realized since Flight 1380 is that hope may not change our circumstances, but it always changes *us*.

Hope, like habits, is uniquely human and a gift. Our minds are incredibly powerful, and hope is the glue that holds us together when facts and circumstances could easily tear us apart.

During my SERE School training, I heard story after incredible story of prisoners of war who had survived years of horrid treatment. What pulled them through? It wasn't hatred for their enemies. They didn't sit around plotting revenge, which can rot a person from within. Instead, the POWs who focused on something beyond their immediate circumstances got through each day. One gentleman played golf in his mind, imagining each swing at each hole. Another made a spider his pet. He fed and protected it. Playing mental golf, caring for that spider, focusing on something other than themselves became something the POWs could look forward to when their surroundings were unbearable.

> Hope may not change our circumstances, but it always changes us.

Hope, even in a tiny dose, is powerful. My flight students worried about the frightening feeling of their aircraft stalling during their out-of-control flight. But my advice that they eat a peanut butter sandwich, along with my promise that we could do acrobatics when we finished, took their minds off getting sick and gave them something to look forward to.

That day on Flight 1380, when Darren and I agreed that Philadelphia was the best place to land, our perspective on our bad situation shifted. We had a destination. We had hope. Darren and I could start working on a plan. We shared that plan with our passengers. Now people knew that we weren't in a free fall. Hope took our minds out of the what-if scenarios and kept us on the problem-solving track. Hope helped us do our best thinking.

What hope keeps you going when you're worried about something? Do you take time to share your good idea with others? It could be helpful.

The third truth is that heroes don't require special equipment or superpowers. They don't need to land a crippled plane. A true hero is someone who takes the time to see and the effort to act for someone else's good. In a word, they *care*.

A lump still comes to my throat when I think of the passengers who acted so boldly and selflessly during the crisis of Flight 1380. When I came out of the cockpit, I observed the way strangers were treating each other with the tenderness of a family. Later I learned more about what the flight attendants and other passengers had done. All kind gestures matter, big or small. Before everyone got off the plane, one passenger helped another tie her shoes. That simple act of meeting a need is heroic in my eyes.

Among my own heroes are people such as my dad, who passed away while I was writing this book. My daddy encouraged me to tackle the nonsense in my path rather than avoid it. My mom is my hero for too many reasons to list (as well as being the most selfless cheerleader I know). Captain Rosemary Mariner was a mentor and friend who helped people like me by creating new opportunities for us. And the amazing man I married, Dean, is a hero whose selflessness has made our marriage and our family strong.

If you want to be a hero, all you have to do is pay attention. When you see that someone needs help, help them without being asked.

My dream of flying was only the starting pistol that launched me into the race of my life. The years of hard work that followed put me in the right place at the right time, preparing me to be the captain of Flight 1380.

You might recall that when I was still at the dreaming stage of aviation, in high school, I ran across the poem "To a Waterfowl" by William Cullen Bryant. His family and friends had urged him to become a teacher or lawyer, but he wanted to be a writer. He was torn about what to do, but his heart was calmed when he saw some geese flying south for the winter. He realized we were each made for what we should do, and he wrote this poem:

> He, who, from zone to zone,
> Guides through the boundless sky thy certain
>   flight,
> In the long way that I must trace alone,
> Will lead my steps aright.

Bryant became a poet, a writer, and an editor who mentored other writers and had a profound impact on American literature. In the end, dreams aren't always just about us. But they start within our own hearts and minds, and they can send us on journeys that change our lives, and others' lives, for the better.

Blessings in your adventures ahead.

With joy,

Captain Tammie Jo Shults

| Apt Elev | 36 | | | | | |

MALSR

MISSED APPROACH: C...
1500 then climbing righ...
3000 on MXE VORTAC
to MXE VORTAC and he...

Requires specific OPSPEC, MSPEC or LOA approval and use of HUD to DH.
Reduced lighting: requires specific OPSPEC, MSPEC or LOA
...nd use of autoland or HUD to touchdown.

A5

PHILADELPHIA APP CON	PHILADELPHIA TOWER		GND CON	CLN...
124.35 319.15	118.5 327.05 (Rwys 9L/27R, 8/26 and 17/35)		121.9 348.6	118.85
	135.1 327.05 (Rwy 9R/27L)			CPE...

Procedure NA for arrivals at
MENGE on V479 northbound.

A 1547

(IAF)
MENGE
ARD 15

108.2 ARD
Chan 19

3000
200°
(5.1)

Procedure NA for arriva...
at ENZEW on V123-15...
northeast bound.

LOCALIZER 108.95
I-PDP
Chan 26 (Y)

MISSED
APCH FIX

3000
268°
(5.5)

088°

A (IAF)
ENZEW
RBV 23.1

A 1153 ±

NAAS Mustin
(Abandoned)

432 A

216 270
A

388

617
A

2100
268°
(5.1)

(IF)
MRTIN INT
I-PDP 11.3

R-200

JALTO
I-PDP 6.1

199
A

246
A

A 281

184 A

A 278

284

E

ALTERNATE ...
APCH FIX

POTTSTOWN...
PTW
116.5
Chan 112

...OD 25 NM

...600

A 1055

ELEV 36

D TDZ...

141

WOODSTOWN
112.8 OOD
Chan 75

3000

MXE

MXE
R-115

VGSI and ILS glidepath not coincident
(VGSI Angle 3.00/TCH 81).

JALTO
I-PDP 6.1

2100

MRTIN INT
I-PDP 11.3

3000

A5

A4

A5

A 112 ±

TW

14...

I-PDP
DME ANTENNA

268°

2100

GS 3.00°
TCH 52

181'

	A	B	C	D
...6.3 NM		...5.1 NM		

...ORY

SA CAT I RA 157/14 150 DA 161

7R

SA CAT II RA 102/12 100 DA 111

GLOSSARY

adrenaline—a stress-induced hormone that causes an increased heart rate

aerobatics—specialized flying that involves maneuvers such as rolls and dives

aerodynamics—the study of how a plane's wings, flaps, tail, and body help create lift in the air

ailerons—flight controls that cause an aircraft to roll

aviator—pilot

bogey—possible enemy aircraft

bow—the front part of a boat

brief—a meeting to plan or review a flight or mission

cabin—the passenger area of an airplane

catapult—a device for hurling heavy objects great distances

cat shot—a takeoff from an aircraft carrier, in which the plane is launched from the catapult

civilian—a person who is not on active duty with a military

cockpit—the space on an aircraft where pilots sit and operate the plane

commercial airline—planes operated by a private company rather than by the military, usually to transport passengers

commission—an earned certificate granting the rank of an officer in the military

cowling—the frame that surrounds the engine of a plane

CPR—cardiopulmonary resuscitation; an emergency procedure to help someone whose heartbeat or breathing has stopped

depressurization—the loss of air pressure

drag—force from wind or air that opposes a moving object

enlisted—military troops with a rank below that of an officer

flight surgeon—military doctor for pilots

formation flying—flying in tight shapes with other planes

galley—the area of an airplane where flight attendants prepare food and drinks

glide slope—the path of descent an airplane must follow to make a safe landing

hangar—a large building where airplanes are housed or repaired

hydraulics—a system of hoses or tubes that convey liquids to an engine's hydraulic system; hydraulic systems help steer and land airplanes

jump seat—a folding seat used by flight attendants for take-off and landing

lift—the force that keeps a plane in the air, created mostly by the wings as the plane moves through the atmosphere

meatball—a light system that lets pilots know if they're on the proper path to land

med down—temporarily unable to fly due to a medical condition

meteorology—the study of weather

navigation—finding your way safely from one point to another

radar—the use of radio waves to locate the position and movement of objects, such as planes and boats

ready room—the pilots' breakroom

recruiter—a person who helps civilians enlist in the military

rudder—a flat hinged panel on the back of a plane that steers by turning against the air current

simulator—a training device that imitates different conditions and actions associated with operating a vehicle

sortie—a flight

squadron—a local military unit, typically one associated with aircraft

starboard—the right side of a boat

stern—the back end of a boat

tactical aircraft—planes capable of attack with guns, bombs, or missiles

throttle—a lever that controls fuel flow to an engine; moving the throttle changes a vehicle's speed

thrust—the force that moves a vehicle along its path of motion, usually created by an engine

TOPGUN—United States Navy Strike Fighter Tactics Instructor program; a training program for the Navy's

best jet pilots; formerly named Navy Fighter Weapons
School

touch-and-go—a training exercise to practice landing a
plane; the pilot touches the landing gear to the runway,
then takes off again without coming to a stop

trapping—landing a plane on an aircraft carrier by catching
the plane's tailhook on a cable

wingman—a pilot who follows the lead pilot in formation
flying

SIDEBAR SOURCES

Chapter 3: What Is Dogfighting?

"Flight Training Instruction." *Aviation Maintenance and Training, Volume 2*. Integrated Publishing, Inc. http://navyflightmanuals.tpub.com/P-821/.

Chapter 5: Women with Wings

"Air Force ROTC." Today's Military. https://www.todaysmilitary.com/education-training/rotc-programs#jump-air-force-rotc.

DiMascio, Jen. "When the Pentagon First Let Women Fly in Combat (1993)." Aviation Week Network. April 28, 2015. https://aviationweek.com/blog/when-pentagon-first-let-women-fly-combat-1993.

Eckstein, Megan. "Navy to Honor First Female Fighter Pilot with Female-Piloted Flyover at Funeral." *USNI News*. January 30, 2019. https://news.usni.org/2019/01/30/navy-honor-first-female-fighter-pilot-female-piloted-flyover-funeral.

"Employment Benefits." Today's Military. https://www
.todaysmilitary.com/careers-benefits/employment
-benefits.

"Explore Careers." Today's Military. https://www
.todaysmilitary.com/careers-benefits/explore-careers.

"Frequently Asked Questions (FAQ)." Today's Military.
https://www.todaysmilitary.com/faq.

"From Typewriters to Strike Fighters: Women in Naval
Aviation." National Naval Aviation Museum. https://
www.navalaviationmuseum.org/education/online
-exhibits/typewriters-strike-fighters-women-naval
-aviation/.

Ganson, Barbara. "U.S. Women of Military Aviation History
Since World War I." Women of Aviation Worldwide Week.
Institute for Women of Aviation Worldwide. February 21,
2015. https://web.archive.org/web/20161226161804/http://
www.womenofaviationweek.org/u-s-women-of-military
-aviation-history-since-world-war-i/.

Garwood, Barbara. "History of the Women Military
Aviators." Women Military Aviators, Inc. http://www
.womenmilitaryaviators.org/history-of-wma.html.

Goldstein, Richard. "Rosemary Mariner, Pathbreaking Navy
Pilot and Commander, Is Dead at 65." *New York Times*.
February 1, 2019. https://www.nytimes.com/2019/02/01
/obituaries/rosemary-mariner-dead.html.

Johnson, Caroline. "Women with Wings: The 75-Year-Legacy
of the WASP." Smithsonian National Air and Space
Museum. August 5, 2018. https://airandspace.si.edu
/stories/editorial/women-wings-75-year-legacy-wasp.

Kennedy, Kelly. "What It Was Like to Be One of the First
Female Fighter Pilots." *New York Times*. May 2, 2018.
https://www.nytimes.com/2018/05/02/magazine/women
-pilots-military.html.

Martin, Hugo. "Women Pioneers of Aviation to Be Saluted at Airport Expo." *Los Angeles Times*. August 21, 1993. https://www.latimes.com/archives/la-xpm-1993-08-21-me-26064-story.html.

Peach, Lucinda J. *Women at War: The Ethics of Women in Combat*. Bloomington, IN: Indiana Center on Global Change and World Peace, Indiana University, 1993. https://heinonline.org/HOL/LandingPage?handle=hein.journals/hplp15&div=15&id=&page=.

Rickman, Sarah Byrn. "A History of the Women Airforce Service Pilots." National WASP WWII Museum. https://waspmuseum.org/.

Texas Woman's University Libraries. "Training." Women Airforce Service Pilots (WASP). https://web.archive.org/web/20180728221611/https://twu.edu/library/womans-collection/featured-collections/women-airforce-service-pilots-wasp/training/.

Texas Woman's University Libraries. "Women Airforce Service Pilots Digital Archive." Gateway to Women's History. https://web.archive.org/web/20161104001523/http://twudigital.cdmhost.com/cdm/landingpage/collection/p214coll2.

"Thune Recognizes Women Airforce Service Pilots from World War II." June Thune, U.S. Senator for South Dakota. May 21, 2009. https://web.archive.org/web/20181224124130/https://www.thune.senate.gov/public/index.cfm/press-releases?ID=026B5888-86E0-4688-A4FC-E9E680EA96E4.

"Timeline of Women in the US Navy." United States Navy Personnel Command. https://web.archive.org/web/20160520111650/http://www.public.navy.mil/bupers-npc/organization/bupers/WomensPolicy/Pages/HistoryFirsts.aspx.

Wilson, Barbara A. "Military Women Pilots." Military
    Women Veterans. AUG LINK Communications, Inc.
    http://userpages.aug.com/captbarb/pilots.html.
Women in Aviation International. "Current Statistics of
    Women in Aviation Careers in U.S." https://www.wai.org
    /resources/waistats.
Women in Military Service for America Memorial
    Foundation, Inc. "Highlights in the History of Military
    Women." The Women's Memorial. https://www
    .womensmemorial.org/content/resources/highlights.pdf.

Chapter 6: What Is ROTC?

US Army. "Army ROTC: College Scholarship FAQ." Updated
    October 12, 2018. https://www.goarmy.com/rotc/college
    -students/faq.html#WhatareArmy.
US Army. "Earn Your Degree Through ROTC." Updated
    November 1, 2018. https://www.goarmy.com/benefits
    /education-benefits/earn-your-degree-through-rotc.html.
US Army. "Officer: Frequently Asked Questions." Updated
    October 12, 2018. https://www.goarmy.com/careers-and
    -jobs/become-an-officer/army-officer-faqs.html.
US Army. "Service Commitment." Army ROTC. Updated
    September 17, 2018. https://www.goarmy.com/rotc
    /service-commitment.html.

Chapter 9: Tammie Jo's Planes

"1968 Cessna 177 Cardinal." CESSNA Models. Planephd.
    https://planephd.com/wizard/details/203/CESSNA-177
    -Cardinal-specifications-performance-operating-cost
    -valuation.

Alex, Dan. "Beechcraft T-34 Mentor: Basic Trainer/Light
    Attack Aircraft." MilitaryFactory.com. Updated
    August 7, 2018. https://www.militaryfactory.com
    /aircraft/detail.asp?aircraft_id=778.
Aviastar. "Vought A-7 Corsair II (USA) (1965)." The
    -Blueprints.com. https://www.the-blueprints.com
    /blueprints/modernplanes/vought/35981/view
    /vought_a_7_corsair_ii__usa___1965_/.
"Beechcraft T 34 Mentor." The-Blueprints.com. https://
    www.the-blueprints.com/blueprints/modernplanes
    /beechcraft/2033/view/beechcraft_t_34_mentor/.
"Beechcraft T-34 Mentor Trainer Aircraft." Air Force
    Technology. https://www.airforce-technology.com
    /projects/t-34-trainer/.
"Boeing F/A-18 Super Hornet: Carrier-based Strike Fighter
    Aircraft." Military Factory. Updated April 3, 2019.
    https://www.militaryfactory.com/aircraft/detail
    .asp?aircraft_id=257.
"Cardinal 177: Aircraft Performance Specifications."
    Cardinal Flyers Online. https://www.cardinalflyers.com
    /prep/specs/177.php.
"Cessna 177 Cardinal." Aircraft Owners and Pilots
    Association. https://www.aopa.org/go-fly/aircraft-and
    -ownership/aircraft-fact-sheets/cessna-177-cardinal.
"Cessna 177 Cardinal." The-Blueprints.com. https://www
    .the-blueprints.com/vectordrawings/show/4345/cessna
    _177_cardinal/.
"Cessna 177 Cardinal History, Performance and
    Specifications." Pilot Friend. http://www.pilotfriend
    .com/aircraft%20performance/Cessna/C177%20
    cardinal.htm.
"Cessna 177 Cardinal – Performance Data." RisingUp
    Aviation. https://www.risingup.com/planespecs/info
    /airplane277.shtml.

"Cessna O-2A Skymaster." National Museum of the United States Air Force. May 18, 2015. https://www .nationalmuseum.af.mil/Visit/Museum-Exhibits/Fact -Sheets/Display/Article/196063/cessna-o-2a-skymaster/.

"Cessna O-2 Skymaster." Cactus Air Force Wings and Wheels Museum. http://www.cactusairforce.com /inventory_item/cessna-o2-skymaster/.

"Cessna O-2 Skymaster: Observation Platform Aircraft." Military Factory. https://www.militaryfactory.com /aircraft/detail.asp?aircraft_id=947.

Davisson, Budd. "Flying the Charlie Model Mentor, When It Was Brand New." Airbum.com. http://www.airbum.com /pireps/PirepT34C.html.

"Douglas A-4 Skyhawk: Light Attack Multirole Carrier -Borne Fighter Aircraft." Military Factory. Updated January 28, 2019. https://www.militaryfactory.com /aircraft/detail.asp?aircraft_id=165.

Ferriere, Richard. "Cessna 177 Cardinal." The-Blueprints .com. https://www.the-blueprints.com/blueprints /modernplanes/cessna/46854/view/cessna_177_cardinal/.

"LTV A-7 Corsair II: Carrier-Borne Strike Aircraft." Military Factory. Updated May 25, 2019. https://www .militaryfactory.com/aircraft/detail.asp?aircraft_id=116.

"McDonnell Douglas A-4 Skyhawk." The-Blueprints.com. https://www.the-blueprints.com/blueprints /modernplanes/mcdonnell-douglas/45957/view /mcdonnell_douglas_a_4_skyhawk/.

"Mcdonnell Douglas Fa18 Hornet, General Dynamics F16 Fighting Falcon, Mcdonnell Douglas F15 Eagle, Silhouette." KissPNG.com. https://www.kisspng.com /png-mcdonnell-douglas-f-a-18-hornet-general -dynamics-f-1980644/preview.html.

"North American/Boeing T-2 Buckeye: Naval Jet Trainer Aircraft." Military Factory. Updated August 2, 2017.

https://www.militaryfactory.com/aircraft/detail.asp ?aircraft_id=329.

Palt, Karsten. "Boeing 737-700: Airliner." Flugzeug. http://www.flugzeuginfo.net/acdata_php/acdata_7377_en.php.

Saranga, Dan. "Boeing 737-700." The-Blueprints.com. https://www.the-blueprints.com/blueprints/modernplanes/boeing/73449/view/boeing_737_700/.

Saranga, Dan. "McDonnell Douglas FA-18 Hornet." The-Blueprints.com. https://www.the-blueprints.com/blueprints/modernplanes/mcdonnell-douglas/41399/view/mcdonnell_douglas_fa_18_hornet/.

Saranga, Dan. "North American T-2 Buckeye." The-Blueprints.com. https://www.the-blueprints.com/blueprints/modernplanes/north-american/85752/view/north_american_t_2_buckeye/.

"Vought A-7 Corsair II Attack Fighter." Aircraft Museum. Updated March 17, 2012. http://www.aerospaceweb.org/aircraft/attack/a7/.

Chapter 12: US Navy Officer Rank Structure

"Ensign." Encyclopædia Britannica. January 5, 2017. https://www.britannica.com/topic/ensign-military-rank.

"Rank Insignia of the U.S. Armed Forces: Officers." Aviation Explorer. http://www.aviationexplorer.com/air_force_rank_structure.htm.

Chapter 15: Women in Combat

"A History of Women in the U.S. Military." Infoplease. https://www.infoplease.com/us/military-affairs/history-women-us-military.

"Anna Maria Lane." *History of Women.* http://www
.womenhistoryblog.com/2011/07/anna-maria-lane
-soldier.html.

"Anna Maria Lane." In *An Encyclopedia of American
Women at War: From the Home Front to the
Battlefields,* Lisa Tendrich Frank, ed. Vol. 1, A-L. Santa
Barbara, CA: ABC-CLIO, 2013.

Brown, Nona. "The Armed Forces Find Woman 'Has' a
Place." *New York Times.* December 26, 1948.

Colonial Williamsburg Foundation, The. "Time Line:
Women in the U.S. Military." https://www.history.org
/history/teaching/enewsletter/volume7/images/nov
/women_military_timeline.pdf.

Dever, Mary. "With Historic Number of Women in Uniform,
the Vet Community Is About to Change." Military.com.
March 11, 2019. https://www.military.com/daily-news
/2019/03/11/historic-number-women-uniform-vet
-community-about-change.html.

Ebbert, Jean, and Marie-Beth Hall. "Women in the Navy."
Vietnam Women's Memorial Foundation. http://www
.vietnamwomensmemorial.org/pdf/jebbert.pdf.

Granville, Anna. "American Women Who Served in Combat
Before You Were Born." *Task & Purpose.* November 11,
2015. https://taskandpurpose.com/american-women
-who-served-in-combat-before-you-were-born.

Howat, Kenna. "Mythbusting the Founding Mothers."
National Women's History Museum. July 14, 2017.
https://www.womenshistory.org/articles/mythbusting
-founding-mothers.

"How Roles Have Changed for Women in the Military."
Norwich University Online. November 26, 2018. https://
online.norwich.edu/academic-programs/resources/how
-roles-have-changed-for-women-in-the-military.

Maranzani, Barbara. "Harriet Tubman's Daring Raid, 150 Years Ago." History.com. May 31, 2013. https://www.history.com/news/harriet-tubmans-daring-raid-150-years-ago.

Massey, Mary Elizabeth. *Women in the Civil War*. Lincoln, NE: University of Nebraska Press, 1966.

Myers, Meghann. "Almost 800 Women Are Serving in Previously Closed Army Combat Jobs. This Is How They're Faring." *Army Times*. October 9, 2018. https://www.armytimes.com/news/your-army/2018/10/09/almost-800-women-are-serving-in-previously-closed-army-combat-jobs-this-is-how-theyre-faring/.

Raphel, Alexandra. "Women in the U.S. Military and Combat Roles: Research Roundup." Journalist's Resource. January 23, 2014. https://journalistsresource.org/studies/society/gender-society/women-military-research-roundup/.

"Resources—Historical Frequently Asked Questions." Women in Military Service for America Memorial Foundation, Inc. https://www.webcitation.org/6HZXQsuPG?url=http://www.womensmemorial.org/H%26C/Resources/hfaq.html.

Siemaszko, Corky. "All-Female Air Force Team, the 'Strike Eagles of 'Dudette '07', Make History on Afghanistan Mission." *Daily News*. April 4, 2011. https://www.nydailynews.com/news/national/all-female-air-force-team-strike-eagles-dudette-07-history-afghanistan-mission-article-1.108763.

"Timeline of Women in the US Navy." US Navy Personnel Command. https://web.archive.org/web/20160520111650/http://www.public.navy.mil/bupers-npc/organization/bupers/WomensPolicy/Pages/HistoryFirsts.aspx.

Wilson, Barbara A. "Operation Desert Fox." Military
    Women Veterans. http://userpages.aug.com/captbarb
    /fox.html.
"Women in the Civil War." History.com. February 5, 2010.
    https://www.history.com/topics/american-civil-war
    /women-in-the-civil-war.

Chapter 18: What Are the Blue Angels?

"Frequently Asked Questions." United State Navy. https://
    www.blueangels.navy.mil/faq/
"History of the Blue Angels." United State Navy. https://
    www.blueangels.navy.mil/history/
Tallman, Jill W. "'Fat albert' Pilot: Capt. Katie Higgins the
    Blue Angels' First Female Pilot." AOPA Foundation.
    https://www.aopa.org/news-and-media/all-news/2016
    /september/pilot/capt-katie-higgins

Chapter 22: Flight 1380 Path

Bacon, John. "Mother of Two Dies in Mid-Air Crisis
    After Being Wedged in Southwest Plane Window."
    USA Today. April 17, 2018. https://www.usatoday
    .com/story/news/nation/2018/04/17/southwest
    -flight-makes-emergency-landing-philadelphia
    /524503002/.
"Flightradar24 Data Related to Southwest Airlines Flight
    1380." Flightradar 24, April 19, 2018. https://www
    .flightradar24.com/blog/flightradar24-data-related-to
    -southwest-airlines-flight-1380/.

Chapter 23: Is It Safe to Fly?

Munro, Kelsey. "How Safe Is Flying? Here's What the Statistics Say." *SBS News*. July 31, 2018. https://www.sbs.com.au/news/how-safe-is-flying-here-s-what-the-statistics-say.

Negroni, Christine. "Why Airplanes Are Safe." *Travel + Leisure*. February 2, 2017. https://www.travelandleisure.com/articles/why-airplanes-are-safe.

MALSR

MISSED APPROACH: C
1500 then climbing rig
3000 on MXE VORTAC
to MXE VORTAC and h

Requires specific OPSPEC, MSPEC or LOA approval and use of HUD to DH.
Reduced lighting: requires specific OPSPEC, MSPEC or LOA
and use of autoland or HUD to touchdown.

Ⓐ5

PHILADELPHIA APP CON	PHILADELPHIA TOWER	GND CON	CLN
124.35 319.15	118.5 327.05 (Rwys 9L/27R, 8/26 and 17/35) 135.1 327.05 (Rwy 9R/27L)	121.9 348.6 118.85	CP

∧1547

Procedure NA for arrivals at
MENGE on V479 northbound.

(IAF)
MENGE
ARD 15

108.2 ARD
Chan 19

Procedure NA for arriv
at ENZEW on V123-15
northeast bound.

MISSED
APCH FIX

LOCALIZER 108.95
I-PDP
Chan 26 (Y)

3000
200°
(5.1)

3000
268°
(5.5)

088°

(IAF)
ENZEW
RBV 23.1

∧1153 ±

NAAS Mustin
(Abandoned)

432 ∧

216 ∧

270

388 ∧

617 ∧

2100
268°
(5.1)

R-200

(IF)
MRTIN INT
I-PDP 11.3

246

199

184 ∧

281 ∧

JALTO
I-PDP 6.1

∧278

∧284

ALTERNATE
APCH FIX

POTTSTOW
PTW
116.5
Chan 112

OD 25 NM

2600

∧1055

WOODSTOWN
112.8 OOD
Chan 75

ELEV 36

D TD

VGSI and ILS glidepath not coincident
(VGSI Angle 3.00/TCH 81).

3000

MXE

MXE
R-115

JALTO
I-PDP 6.1

MRTIN INT
I-PDP 11.3

141
☆

2100

268°

3000

A4

I-PDP
DME ANTENNA

2100

A5

GS 3.00°
TCH 52

12000 X 200

112 ±

6.3 NM

5.1 NM

TW
14

1181'

ORY

A

B

C

D

27R

SA CAT I RA 157/14 150 DA 161

ABOUT THE AUTHOR

Captain Tammie Jo Shults is a Southwest Airline captain and former naval aviator. She received wide acclaim when, on April 17, 2018, she and her crew successfully landed a Boeing 737 after one engine exploded and a broken window caused the plane to lose air pressure, saving the lives of 148 people. Shults's early interest in flying led her to become one of the first female F/A-18 Hornet pilots in the United States Navy after overcoming several obstacles due to her gender. Her incredible talent and notable history have made her an inspiration to many.

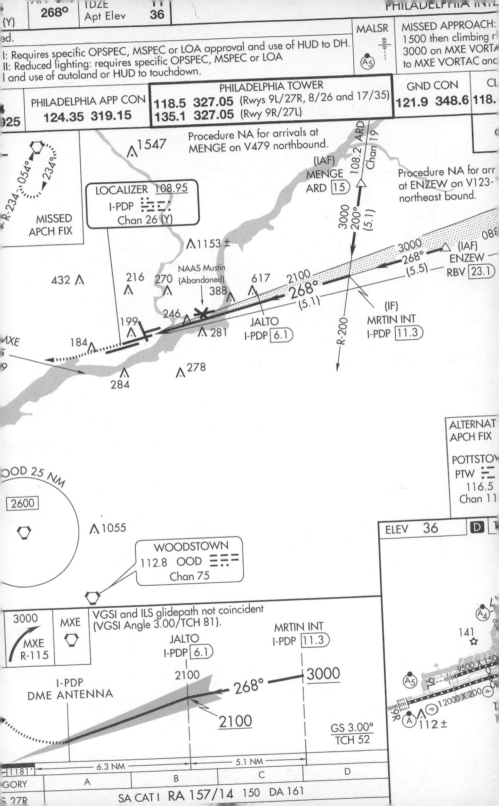

(Y) | 268° | IDZE | 11 | PHILADELPHIA INTL
Apt Elev | 36

...ed.

I: Requires specific OPSPEC, MSPEC or LOA approval and use of HUD to DH.
II: Reduced lighting: requires specific OPSPEC, MSPEC or LOA
I and use of autoland or HUD to touchdown.

MALSR

MISSED APPROACH:
1500 then climbing r...
3000 on MXE VORTA...
to MXE VORTAC an...

PHILADELPHIA APP CON
124.35 319.15

PHILADELPHIA TOWER
118.5 327.05 (Rwys 9L/27R, 8/26 and 17/35)
135.1 327.05 (Rwy 9R/27L)

GND CON
121.9 348.6

CL
118.

...925

Procedure NA for arrivals at
MENGE on V479 northbound.

∧1547

R-234---054°
234°

MISSED
APCH FIX

LOCALIZER 108.95
I-PDP
Chan 26 (Y)

∧1153 ±

NAAS Mustin
(Abandoned)

432 ∧

216 ∧   270 ∧   388
246
199 ∧

∧ 617

2100
268°
(5.1)

MXE

184∧
6
9

∧ 281

∧ 278
∧ 284

JALTO
I-PDP 6.1

108.2 ARD
Chan 19

(IAF)
MENGE
ARD 15

3000
200°
(5.1)

R-200

(IF)
MRTIN INT
I-PDP 11.3

3000
268°
(5.5)

088

(IAF)
ENZEW
RBV 23.1

Procedure NA for arr...
at ENZEW on V123-...
northeast bound.

OOD 25 NM

2600

∧1055

WOODSTOWN
112.8 OOD
Chan 75

ALTERNAT
APCH FIX

POTTSTO...
PTW
116.5
Chan 11

ELEV 36 D

3000
MXE
R-115

MXE

VGSI and ILS glidepath not coincident
(VGSI Angle 3.00/TCH 81).

JALTO
I-PDP 6.1
2100

I-PDP
DME ANTENNA

268°
2100

MRTIN INT
I-PDP 11.3

3000

GS 3.00°
TCH 52

141
☆

A4

A5

9500 X 15...

12000 X 200

A
112 ±

-11181'

GORY

A

B

6.3 NM

C

5.1 NM

D

SA CAT I RA 157/14 150 DA 161

27R